THE BATTLE MAIDENS OF THE LORD

Jacqueline Ethington

ISBN: 978-0-9884436-2-4
LCCN 2012953843.

Published by Linn Neil Publishing,
P.O. Box 748, Mesa, AZ, 85201

Table of Contents

Dedication:

To my beloved husband, children and grandchildren

Introduction

This book has been written to give women courage and hope in this great last battle against Satan and his legions. Women are powerful. God has given his daughters great power. We shall call these valiant women the Battle Maidens of the Lord and their counterparts the Warrior Sons of God.

Some brave souls have agreed to share their stories. All the names have been changed except those from pioneer diaries. All the stories are true and, where possible, are told in the women's own words. Take courage in knowing that great battles are being fought and won. If you have not won your battles yet, *fear not: for they that be with us are more than they that be with them.*[1]

The writings in this book are based on the teachings and principles of the Church of Jesus Christ of Latter-day Saints; however, I do not speak for the church. The gospel of Jesus Christ has been restored in its fullness through the prophet, Joseph Smith, Jr., and the Lord's prophets who have followed him. The Bible, the scriptures of the restoration (<u>Book of Mormon</u>, <u>Doctrine and Covenants</u>, and <u>Pearl of Great Price</u>), and the teachings of prophets and apostles are, for the most part, the basis for the material presented here. Some of the material is founded upon the author's personal experience and the experiences of others and is presented for the reader's consideration.

Chapter 1

The Battle Maidens of the Lord

And there was war in heaven:
Michael and his angels fought against the dragon;
and the dragon fought and his angels, and prevailed not;
neither was their place found any more in heaven.
And the great dragon was cast out,
that old serpent, called the Devil, and Satan,
which deceiveth the whole world:
he was cast out into the earth,
and his angels were cast out with him.[2]

Let us start at the beginning, in an epoch before time. The great Battle Maidens of the Lord and their companions, the valiant Warrior Sons of God including the archangel, Michael, are the defensive forces on the forward front in the longest war in history. This is the war that Satan has been waging against God since the era of the council in Heaven. In the pre-mortal world, these godly fighters infiltrated the enemy lines and brought back untold numbers of God's spirit children captivated by Satan and his clone army. Satan's converts, his comrades in arms, become evil clones of their master. The story of the exploits of the Battle Maidens and the

Jaqueline Ethington

Warrior Sons is an epic tale.

When the Plan of Salvation was presented to the spirit children of our Heavenly Father in the heavenly realms, they rejoiced. They would go to earth to get a body like their heavenly parents and have agency to choose the path they would follow. Their elder brother, Christ, volunteered to go to earth to atone, or pay, for their sins and also bring about the resurrection of their bodies. Because of His sacrifice, all would be able to return to their family in heaven if they repented of their sins. Those who didn't repent of their sins would go to another place that was prepared for them.

At this point, Satan, never one to be outdone, also volunteered to go. Lucifer or Satan was *an angel of God who was in authority in the presence of God.*[3] Probably everyone knew him or knew of him. Of those who seek exalted church positions, he was the ultimate climber. He puffed out his chest and bragged that he wouldn't just save the repentant; he would save everyone. He would destroy the agency of man, which God had given him, and force all to keep the commandments. Therefore, for this great feat, he wanted the Father's glory for himself.

Father chose Christ, the one who was willing to follow His plan, to go and do the saving work for His children so that they could choose to act for themselves and not be compelled to act in ways that Satan would have forced them to act.[4] All of God's children would have the opportunity on earth to choose to follow the Christ and His light that leads to good, or to choose to follow Satan who leads no one to do anything good.

Satan was angry about his Father's choice of

4

Christ and tried to convince the spirit children of God to follow him. He probably played the 'I deserve this promotion' card and 'It just isn't fair' ploy. He bellowed around heaven calling out that his plan was greater because he would save everyone. Perhaps he thought if he went on strike with his sympathizers, he could get management to capitulate. Lucifer did his best to get his brothers and sisters to take the easy way out and follow him. *And he became Satan, yea, even the devil, the father of all lies, to deceive and to blind men, and to lead them captive at his will, even as many as would not hearken unto my voice.*[5]

When the children of God were in heaven, they did not have the earthly experiences that they have now to guide them. They had never been presented with the option of choosing evil, having always lived in a loving and protected environment. In other words, many were childlike beings. Some were confused. Some were fearful of the real possibility of not being able to come back to live with Heavenly Father. Satan's attractive propaganda and glib tongue deceived some into following him, and others were truly rebellious and followed him because they were like him.

Did God let his innocents be thrown out of heaven with the rebellious? No, He did not! *For behold, this is my work and my glory—to bring to pass the immortality and eternal life of man.*[6] The Father wanted all of His children to gain eternal life. He didn't let his children go easily. Under the Father's direction, Christ organized the Father's strongest and most faithful children into a great recovery force to go in among the deceived and reclaim as many as possible.

Jaqueline Ethington

The great Battle Maidens of the Lord and the valiant Warrior Sons of God are those spirits who had a deep conviction of the divinity of the Father's plan. They had an abiding faith in Heavenly Father and Jesus Christ and were filled with a deep love for them and for their brothers and sisters who were deceived by Satan's charismatic personality and persuasive tongue. These courageous children of the Father went into snarling evil and amid devilish dangers to convince their beloved family that they could succeed, that the plan of a loving Father and His Son, Jesus Christ, was designed to lead to glory and even exaltation, and that agency was a blessing, not a curse.

In the pre-mortal world, these Christian soldiers were the ones who inspired others to greater righteousness, greater valor, and greater heights. Others followed where they led because of their ability to light the fire of testimony and help increased faith in God the Father and His Son Jesus Christ. These Battle Maidens and Warrior Sons had the skill to communicate their understanding and burning convictions of gospel truths to others through the power of the Holy Ghost. The Spirit would convey their powerful words into the hearts of their listeners to the convincing of many of the truth and beauty of the Plan of Salvation.

In order to bring the children of God back to Him, the Battle Maidens and the Warrior Sons sought out those who had joined Satan, and with love they reasoned with them to help these children understand the truth and beauty of the Plan of Happiness. They did not stop their efforts until all who would come out, had come

The Battle Maidens of the Lord

out. Or all who could be persuaded had been persuaded of the divinity of the Father's plan. Satan and his followers were not cast out until all who would return to God had returned. It was a perilous assignment. Only the most steadfast went into the company of the deceived.

When the noble ones had finished their work under the direction of Christ, and all who could be saved had returned, leaving only the truly rebellious, Satan was cast out. *And the great dragon was cast out, that old serpent, called the Devil, and Satan, which deceiveth the whole world: he was cast out into the earth, and his angels were cast out with him.*[7]

After the rebellious were banished from heaven, the obedient began the preparation for their life on earth. They had done the will of their Father by seeking to retrieve their lost siblings. Now they continued to emulate their beloved older brother, Jesus Christ. When God asked who He could send into the world to be the savior of the world, Christ said, *Here am I, send me.*[8] The valiant children of God wanted to be like him and volunteered for difficult assignments also. For example, when the Lord needed someone to warn the children of Israel to repent and return to him, Isaiah volunteered. *Also I heard the voice of the Lord, saying, Whom shall I send, and who will go for us? Then said I, Here am I; send me.*[9] When He needed men and women to fulfill difficult assignments, the Battle Maidens and the Warrior Sons are some of the spirit children of God who stepped forward and said, "Here am I, send me." Many of these volunteers were the men and women of the last days. A great many members of the Church of Jesus Christ of Latter-day

7

Saints fall into this category, but also many others. They
would come to earth with spiritual gifts that enabled them
to successfully continue to fight the war that began in
heaven. These sons and daughters of God are among the
great and noble ones. [133]

The Battle Maidens volunteered for some
particularly difficult assignments. There are numerous
examples of women dealing with difficulties in this book.
For example, many women have to deal with rebellious
children. Those couples that take the opportunity to be
married in the temple or to have their families sealed
together in the temple at a later date are blessed indeed.
The parents have been promised that if they remain
faithful that they can retrieve their rebellious children
who don't repent in this life. First those children will
most likely have to deal with the demands of justice after
death, but then through the mercy of God their parents
can go and get them and reunite their families. No
person is a part of this temple sealing covenant by
mistake. It is too rare a gift. It is available to all mankind,
but few will take advantage of it.

There are some children who were extremely
valiant in the war in heaven, but because of their natures,
God knew that they would miss the mark here on earth.
Perhaps they would bring to earth character traits that
they would use for good in the presence of God but might
be corrupted by Satan here on earth. Pride,
determination, a virulent love of agency, or even a great
desire to please others could be some of those traits. Or
perhaps they wouldn't listen closely to the Spirit. God
knew their weaknesses. He wanted them in a place where

The Battle Maidens of the Lord

He could retrieve them after their earth lives through the temple covenants that their parents had made. He asked who would be willing to take these potentially problem children. Some mothers said, "Here am I, send me." These are the children that parents sometimes grieve over because of their choices. Perhaps certain children volunteered for assignments that would be particularly difficult for them such as chronic illness and a willing mother was needed to help them go through their ordeal. Some mothers said, "Here am I, send me."

Heavenly Father needed some women to remain single in order to perform particular missions that married women could not do. He also needed women to adopt unwanted children. There are spirits who were of such a valiant nature that they did not need to prove themselves on earth and only needed to come and get their bodies. They died young, leaving sorrowing parents. To all these mission assignments there were Battle Maidens who said, "Here am I, send me."

Many women said, "Here am I, send me," when the call went out for women to marry and raise families, large and small. As women in the thick of this particular battle know, this is not an easy assignment. These women know that the Lord has not rescinded the commandment to multiply and replenish the earth. Righteous families doing the work of the Lord are Satan's greatest enemies. That is why he is trying so hard to destroy God's pattern for the family. These Battle Maidens steadfastly defend the traditional family unit. Women not engaged in childrearing have other important missions to perform. There are so many different missions for which women

Jaqueline Ethington

said to the Lord, "Here am I, send me."

The Battle Maidens of the Lord, the women who are capable of fulfilling these difficult assignments which will be needed in these days, have been reserved a long time to come to earth to fight this last fierce battle against Satan and his forces. These Battle Maidens are the women who live on the earth in this era. Now is the time when the devil is using his perfected arts. He has had a long time to practice, and God is permitting him to do his evil work. Satan will not be able to say that he never had his chance to practice his agency and do his worst. We all have perfect freedom to choose to listen to Satan. His message is blared everywhere. Or we can choose to follow Christ, whose message is whispered and understood by perceptive and willing hearts.

We, the Battle Maidens of the Lord, have come to earth to fulfill the missions we agreed upon in the pre-mortal world and are following the same pattern set forth in the spirit world. The Prophet Joseph F. Smith saw in vision Christ's work in the spirit world between the time He died on the cross and the time He was resurrected.

I perceived that the Lord went not in person among the wicked and the disobedient who had rejected the truth, to teach them; but behold, from among the righteous, he organized his forces and appointed messengers, clothed with power and authority, and commissioned them to go forth and carry the light of the gospel to them that were in darkness... Among the great and mighty ones who were assembled in this vast congregation of the righteous were Father Adam, the Ancient of Days and father of all, and our glorious Mother Eve, with many of her faithful daughters who had lived through the ages and worshiped the true and living God.[10] And we also, like these glorious daughters of Eve, will continue our missions in the war for salvation when we leave this world and join our battle mates on the other side of the veil.

We have to remember that God is the same yesterday, today and forever.[11] God sent his mighty ones in among the forces of Satan in the pre-mortal world to reason with them and bring back those who could be persuaded to return to Him. He sends His missionaries out into the world today so that humanity might be saved. And after this life, He sends His messengers, both men and women, to teach the gospel to those in spirit prison so that they might be redeemed. These messengers are the valiant Warrior Sons of God and the great Battle Maidens of the Lord.

There are many Battle Maidens on the earth now. God sends more every day, and He will continue to send them until the end of time, when Christ comes in His glory. In this great last battle against evil, the Battle Maidens and the Warrior Sons will fight honorably because that is their nature. These Christian soldiers know the enemy. They have fought him and his legions before and have brought many back to their God. They go to battle again with their ancient battle mates, Christ, family, and friends, and the other valiant souls of the earth. The armies of the Lord don't fight alone, nor do they stop. They persevere in patience and bring back many of God's children who have been led astray by Satan. They seek out those who will accept the Father's plan among their own families and among their associates as the Spirit leads them to do so. This army is us. We are the Battle Maidens of the Lord.

We cry out once again our sacred battle cry. "Christ our Redeemer, Savior and King, be thou with us."

The Lord is teaching his daughters eternal truths. If we listen, He will tell us of our importance and missions in these latter days. We must not quench His Spirit, but listen carefully.[12] The devil desires to have us. So we have to keep the Spirit always with us, living on the Lord's side of the fence, being ever vigilant. Joseph Smith was talking about us, the valiant women, when he said, "If you live up to your privileges, the angels cannot be restrained from being your associates".[13] Those in heaven are watching closely. Angels surround us and give us more aid than we are aware of. When we choose Christ, we are not alone. Heather learned this lesson as a young woman.

One Sunday, Heather was taught by the Spirit how great the souls of the latter day women are and how dearly the Lord values them.

EQUALLY YOKED

A few years back, when I had just had my second child, I was sitting in a Relief Society meeting watching a video of a speech given by Sister Sherry L. Dew of the Relief Society General Presidency. I've since forgotten the contents of that speech, but I know that it concerned the destiny and calling of women. During her talk and the ensuing lesson, I was overcome with the Spirit of the Lord more powerfully than I had ever before been. The teacher was discussing the importance of women in the Lord's plan. Burned into my soul was a message the Lord would not let me keep inside. I've forgotten all the words, but

The Battle Maidens of the Lord
not the meaning of what I said.

"Sometimes I hear women say that they are glad that they don't hold the priesthood because they don't want that kind of responsibility. I believe that is one of Satan's lies. It is a pleasing lie that entices us to think we have been relieved of a heavy burden. Women, and the role they play in the Father's plan, hold no less responsibility than that of men," I said.

"Thank you, Heather," the teacher replied.

The Spirit was burning so powerfully inside of me that I thought every soul in the room would feel its strength.   However, the lesson moved on with little attention paid to my comment. There was no mention of it throughout the remainder of the lesson.

Why had I felt the urgency to say it aloud? As I've thought about it, I believe it was for me more than anyone else. I knew what I said was true. Once I said it aloud, the Lord knew that I understood and had acknowledged the communication.   I realized that if women were to add to their responsibilities that of the priesthood, women would bear by far the greater burden. The yoke between men and women would become unequal.

The Lord taught Heather about the great worth of women and the importance of their particular missions here on earth. The women of the latter days are indeed the great Battle Maidens of the Lord, the ones who fought Satan and his hosts in heaven. We are the ones that God can trust to do the work of preparing the world for the second coming of Christ in great glory. We, the Battle

Jaqueline Ethington

Maidens of the Lord, are standing on the battle lines in real time, fighting to preserve our families and others around us from the evils of the world.

Chapter 2

Battle Lines

For God has not given us the spirit of fear;
But of power, and of love, and of a sound mind
2 Tim. 1:7[14]

The Battle Maidens, and there are many, who are here on earth are equipped to continue the work they began in heaven. They are naturally courageous, especially where their children are concerned. Since they are on the battle lines of life fighting Satan, who is trying to destroy the family, they reason out their plan of action with a sound mind and move forward with power. Now what exactly does that mean? In this chapter there are examples of two women, each from a different time period, reasoning, loving and moving with power to save their family. The following is the story of Ava who lived in a time of war.

TWO TICKETS TO POLAND
Allied bombs fell nightly on Berlin in February of 1944. Every night Ava and her two daughters went to the damp basement to sleep, praying that their neighborhood would not be hit. Four streets away all the houses were in rubble from a bombing raid two nights before. Many residents on that street had escaped to the bomb shelter at Anhalt Station. Some had not.

Jaqueline Ethington

Air raid sirens began to scream into the night, and Ava could hear the drone of planes over the city. Anti-aircraft guns added their tattoo to the music of death. As they fell, the bombs sang a high, shrill note ending in rapid bursts of fire and destruction. The noise was not as loud as usual. Factories in the suburbs were the night's targets.

Yearning for guidance, Ava prayed into the night. Thoughts of her sister in Poland kept coming into her mind. She would send her girls, Heidi and Helga, to her sister. Traveling to Poland was dangerous. Ava thought that the safest way was for her daughters to go by train, and no one had been able to get train tickets for months now.

When morning came, Ava awakened her daughters. "Get up girls and pack your clothes in my old carpet bag. You are going to visit Aunt Gisela."

They arrived at the train station early, but there was already a long line of desperate people. Ava watched as almost everyone was turned away. A fortunate few were allowed through the gate. There was still hope. As Ava got closer she saw that the ticket master was Karl, a member of the SS. She had known him all of her life. He knew just how to flatter and manipulate people in order to get ahead in the world. Now he was manning a railroad ticket window. She wondered why.

Finally, it was Ava's turn at the window. "I need two tickets to Poland for my daughters," she told Karl.

"No," he growled without looking up. "You can't have them. Move along."

The Battle Maidens of the Lord

Ava put her hand under the ticket window, grabbed the man's tie and yanked his shocked face against the glass.

"If my children die," she said, "I will hunt you down." Her low voice pulsed with meaning.

Ava's actions surprised even her, but she received the tickets, and her children lived.

Timidity and fear are not Christ like qualities. Humility, on the other hand, is. The idea is to pray fervently with humility before going to the train station and then act with courage and strength, following the inspiration of the Holy Ghost, once there. Likewise, we cannot be timid and shy in protecting our families from evil. If the devil comes and takes our children down to hell, then we go get them and take them back. That is what we did in the pre-mortal world. We can certainly do our best to do it here, and we can be successful. We need to be strong in the war against evil.

During the War in Heaven, God the Father and Christ sent the Warrior Sons and the Battle Maidens into the ranks of those deceived by Satan to persuade the children of God to come back to the light. They didn't ring their hands and say, "Oh dear. Oh dear. What shall we do? Some of the children have chosen to follow Satan." But rather, they gathered their forces and acted with strength.

The forces of the devil are marshaled and arrayed against the human family. Secret combinations are moving against the peoples of the earth. They delight in turning human life and distress into money and power. Children are being approached at younger and younger ages to try drugs. The airways are filled with pornography, murders, and sins of all kinds. As children of God, we need to do whatever we can to fight for our families, our God, and our nation. We are not defenseless. We have God on our side. *Pray always, that you may come off conqueror; yea, that you may conquer Satan, and that you may escape the hands of the servants of Satan that do uphold his work.*[15]

The battle lines are all around. They are as close as the television in the family room, as everyday as school and work, and as insidious as billboards, magazines and internet pornography. They are as enticing as the clothing store, as mean as a bully, and as capricious as peer pressure.

The following story is of Betty who stands bravely on the battle lines, fighting with courage and determination, taking Christ as her guide.

THE SHOES OF DESTINY

We had some heartache with one of our children. We had some with each one actually. I remember saying to myself, "I think I could handle anything but a child falling away from the church. I'm sure that the Lord wouldn't give me that because that is what I couldn't handle." I remember verbalizing that. Guess what? That is what I got.

In high school, our daughter, Cassidy, started hanging around with some friends that were not doing what was right. She started using marijuana, drinking

The Battle Maidens of the Lord

alcohol, and being rebellious. After graduation, she went to Ricks College in Idaho and got kicked out that spring, two weeks before the end of the semester.

When she came home, the heartache was indescribable. That was one of my darkest, darkest days. The only place I could find peace and solace was in the scriptures.

My husband put his arm around me and said, "Betty, we'll get through this together. Now let's get on the same page and decide what we want to do about it."

Soon after she returned home, she ran away. I didn't know if we would ever see her again. But four months later we went to general conference in Salt Lake City, and she was there. When she saw me, she told me that she liked my shoes.

"Well, if you will promise me you'll go to church, I'll give them to you," I said.

We prayed that the Lord would put somebody in her way that would change her heart. That is exactly what happened. She went back to college at another school and got a great roommate who was the Relief Society President at church. She came back to the church and to her family. Shortly after this, she met her husband. She has done just beautifully since that time. I think the prayers of all her sisters and brothers helped. Now when she talks to young women, she tells this story and brings the shoes.

"My mom got me back to church because of a pair of shoes," she tells them. We later asked her what actually brought her back to the church.

"You just loved me. You didn't tell me I was doing anything wrong. You just loved me," she said.

19

Jaqueline Ethington

That was all we could do at the time. It wouldn't have done any good to tell her what she should do. She knew. We knew she had a strong testimony of the gospel. Her spiritual gift is like mine. We know that Jesus is the Christ. She was unhappy because she was not living the way she knew she should. Now she is a Stake Relief Society President and is doing well with her family.

Betty approached the throne of God on behalf of Cassidy through prayer and scripture study. She received help and inspiration in her struggle to bring a beloved daughter back to family and to Christ. Not everyone's inspiration will be the same as Betty's. Each of us has to seek our own direction from God.

Many women stand on the battle lines between good and evil, fighting for their families and the principles of righteousness. Satan is trying hard to destroy the family, the basic fighting unit for good. If the family is strong and the children are brought up with faith in God and taught to have strong moral standards, they become a strong force against evil. Therefore the destruction of the family is paramount in the devil's plan to destroy the kingdom of God and the civilization of nations. The members of strong families have important missions to perform on earth that Satan would like to stop. The Battle Maidens find themselves more and more on the battle lines defending their positions as faithful mothers and righteous daughters of the Most High who are raising valuable children. They move forward to fulfill their missions sometimes against public ridicule and animosity.

Chapter 3

Missions

*For behold, again I say unto you that if ye will enter in by the
way, And receive the Holy Ghost,
It will show unto you all things what ye should do*

2 Nephi 32:5[16]

IT'S NOT TOO LATE

Melissa raised her children, and when they had all
left home, she became quite despondent. One Sunday
she talked with a young friend after church.

"What do you do during the day?" she asked
Brenda.

"Well, I take care of my little children, clean the
house, do the laundry, that kind of thing," replied
Brenda.

"Doesn't that bother you to do only that?" Melissa
asked.

"It used to, but it doesn't any more. I really enjoy
what I'm doing," said Brenda.

"What else do you do? What interests do you
have?" Melissa seemed interested in Brenda's life, so
Brenda continued.

"I really like to write stories. I've always got a story
going around in my head, but I hardly ever have time to
put it down on paper."

Jaqueline Ethington

"Oh, you should write stories, Brenda. You should write. If you have a talent, you need to develop it," she said. "When I was a mom with young kids, I didn't do that. I just stayed at home, raised my children, did housework and things related to my home. I thought I was being a good mom. But now I just wish I had done something with my talents."

"It's not too late. You have all sorts of time now. What did you want to do? What are your interests? What are your talents?" asked Brenda.

Melissa became emotional. Tears filled her eyes and her voice cracked. "I don't know any more. It has been so long that I've forgotten what my interests used to be. I can't think of anything I would like to do. I don't know what I would find interesting."

Melissa's story is a familiar one. She raised a wonderful, righteous family, and yet she feels like she was cheated in some manner. Nothing could be farther from the truth. Nothing can take this great accomplishment from her. Fame may elude the artist, the writer, or the performer. The CEO of a big company may get fired. The secretary may be demoted to file clerk. But through all eternity, Melissa's work will stand as a testament to her greatness. This certainly does not mean that talents and interests should be put aside. They can add a wonderful dimension to a well-rounded life. But many times other things take priority for a time.

The question that women and in this case, Melissa, should ask is not "What are my talents?" but

22

The Battle Maidens of the Lord

rather, "What are my missions?" What are the missions we were ordained to do here on earth in the pre-mortal world? We should ask the Lord what he would have us do, and then seek for the answer. It takes time and experience to gain the wisdom to fulfill some of our missions. When we have discovered what our present mission is and commence to do it, the Lord will provide the talent for that mission. When we complete one mission, God will send us another. Before long we will be amazed at how talented we have become.

Many, perhaps most of these missions, will be in addition to our church assignments. Church assignments are indeed missions, but there are other responsibilities that women promised to fulfill in the pre-mortal world. "In the world before we came here, faithful women were given certain assignments".[17] Notice the plural nature of "assignments."

And all this for the benefit of the church of the living God, that every man (woman) may improve upon his (her) talent, that every man *(woman) may gain other talents, yea, even an hundred fold, to be cast into the Lord's storehouse, to become the common property of the whole church.*[18] Those who write songs or books that all may enjoy, or speak with the Spirit to touch our hearts through lessons and talks in church, or donate of their means that the poor may be equal in temporal things, or in many other ways, contribute to the common property of the whole church.

Women have many different works to do while they are upon the earth. Their most important assignments will be with their families, but they will have other assignments also. It might be an assignment to befriend another woman. Perhaps a woman will be sent with a message of hope or encouragement for another. Some will be assigned to teach the gospel to someone or to many who have been waiting for it. Maybe a woman's spirit will be calmed so that she is able to sit and listen to someone who needs to talk. Perhaps another woman will write a book, organize a group to fight some evil that is harming their neighborhood or country, cloth the naked, feed the hungry, or paint a beautiful picture to uplift the spirit. If they will listen to the voice of the Spirit, women will have all kinds of loving, friendly tasks to do for the Lord. The missions are so many and so varied that it is impossible to imagine the scope of possibilities. But God knows, and He will tell his daughters what great experiences and assignments He has for them.

The following are stories of people who were prompted to fulfill missions of goodness, love and light. The work of enlightenment was begun in different ages and on different continents. This work of salvation started by these inspired people was continued and built upon by other faithful followers of Christ.

The story of the sons of King Mosiah in the <u>Book of Mormon</u> is a good example of God's servants who fulfilled their highest missions here upon the earth. After repenting of their many sins, the sons of the king rejected an earthly kingdom, wealth and honor, and desired to bring salvation to the Lamanites, their traditional enemies. They could not bear to think of anyone being consigned to spirit prison. After fourteen years of missionary work in the lands of the Lamanites, they brought many people out of a benighted land into the light of the gospel. How great was the joy of these men with their beloved brothers and sisters in the kingdom of our God.[19]

Many years later during Book of Mormon times, about the same time that the Lamanites destroyed the Nephites who had become wicked, God sent another one of his servants to save his people in Ireland. Ireland, at this time, was a collection of warlike petty kingdoms held loosely together by the High King at Tara. Any excuse for a war was acceptable. Having one's honor questioned was an especially popular excuse to go into battle.

The Christian, Patrick, having served as a slave in Ireland for six years, made his escape back to his home in Western Europe. During the years that he had served as a swineherd in Ireland, he had grown close to God, learned the language, and had become Irish at heart. After he returned home, he heard a voice from Ireland calling unto him. "Come to us, O holy youth, and walk among us." He had a mission to teach the Irish the Gospel of Christ. In 432 A.D., he returned to Ireland as a bishop and a great missionary. Even though Patrick did not have the fullness of the restored gospel that we have today, he had the Light of Christ all of the time, and since he was teaching about and testifying of Christ, he very often had the Holy Ghost with him. The understanding that he did have, he shared with the Irish. In one generation the gospel of Christ turned Ireland from a pagan, warlike country into a predominantly God fearing, Christian nation. This was done only with the preaching of the word of God.

Patrick had a mission on earth. I imagine that when the Lord asked the spirits of the pre-mortal world, "Who shall we send to the Irish?" Patrick must have said, "Here am I, send me." He fulfilled his mission faithfully.

Bridget was one of the early Christians in Ireland. She was generous to the poor and kind. She was your basic Relief Society President type. Because of her gentle nature, many of the Irish were converted to Christianity. She also completed her mission here upon the earth faithfully.[20]

The Church of Jesus Christ of Latter-day Saints is growing in Ireland today. A Relief Society President in Dublin called Ireland a holy land. And so it is for the righteous Irish.

During all the ages of man, the Lord has sent his servants to bless his children on the earth. Are these servants among the noble and great ones? Surely they are. There are many of these great spirits upon the earth now, among all nations. Like Mother Teresa in India, they are also here to help prepare the earth for the second coming of Christ in glory. Many of these will accept the restored fullness of the gospel of Jesus Christ when they hear it. Some may never hear it. But because they are the valiant ones who fought for God and Christ in the War in Heaven, they will be a great force for good on the earth and fulfill their missions to prepare the earth for the Lord at His coming. They will gather about them a group of righteous people worthy to meet Christ.

The Battle Maidens of the Lord

Today the gospel is being preached in many lands and the Church is growing in these lands. Before Christ comes, it will be preached in all lands and grow to fill the whole earth. *The keys of the kingdom of God are committed unto man on the earth, and from thence shall the gospel roll forth unto the ends of the earth, as the stone which is cut out of the mountain without hands shall roll forth, until it has filled the whole earth.*[21]

Many people in all nations have magnificent missions to perform here in this mortal realm. The Lord will give them the ability and talents they need to accomplish their missions. The Battle Maidens and the Warrior Sons are all here to further the work of God and prepare for Christ to come again. The army of the Lord is fighting the evil that is slithering across the earth vainly hoping to stop that great day from coming. Whether they recognize it or not, the righteous of the earth who are endeavoring to stem the tide of evil are allies in a great work.

Chapter 4

Allies

And behold, and lo, I am with you
To bless you and deliver you forever
D&C 108:8[22]

The Lord is our ally. He has given His people a great deal of help through the scriptures and prayer, and He is always on call. When there are bewildering problems, the best place to go is the source of all wisdom. Consider the problem and try to figure out what would be a good solution. Then ask the Lord about it. Be humble and ask in mighty prayer. Be patient. He will answer.

At the first sign of trouble, some people tend to fly about like moths headed for a light, any light. Some run to this friend and that stranger for help. There may be some good advice to be had from other people. Consider what they say, but go to the One with the answers. Sometimes it is good to take a calming breath and ask God what should be done, what should be prayed for. God is our ally and friend. *Verily I say unto you my friends, fear not, let your hearts be comforted; yea, rejoice evermore, and in everything give thanks; waiting patiently on the Lord, for your prayers have entered into the ears of the Lord of Sabaoth, and are recorded with his seal and testament—the Lord hath sworn and decreed that they shall be granted. Therefore, he giveth this*

28

promise unto you, with an immutable covenant that they shall be fulfilled; and all things wherewith you have been afflicted shall work together for your good, and to my name's glory, saith the Lord.[23]

When Caroline began to have trouble with her oldest child, she didn't know what to do. She had had no experience to deal with the problems her son was having. This is the story of how she worked with her heavenly and earthly allies to help her son.

A CHANGE OF HEART

When we were having troubles with our son, Derek, I became quite angry with him because he frightened me with his behavior. The drugs he was using and the company he was keeping frightened me. I didn't want to lose him. That fear came out in ways that were not helpful. He accused me of not trusting him, so our conversations weren't very productive.

I prayed about what I should do and began to realize that I needed a change of heart if I was going to be able to help him at all. For quite some time I prayed for that change of heart. I seemed to not be able to control my feelings of anger and fear. That change of heart needed to be a gift in some way because my anger wasn't something that I could overcome on my own.

One day I was sitting in the living room, and he came walking in the house with his bleached hair backlit with the light from the door. At that time the Lord blessed me, and I was able to sense my son's spirit. I didn't see anything in particular, but I sensed this magnificent being. I was overwhelmed with what a beautiful young man he was, and tears filled my eyes. That feeling still stays with me to this day. I don't now feel the intensity that I felt that first time, but every time I'm around him, I'm overwhelmed with who he is. He is just a magnificent man to me. When he walks into a room, it really lights up. That experience changed my heart. After that, I felt honored to be with him.

I realized that he was being controlled by Satan and wasn't himself. He was fighting for his life. At that point, I became very tender towards him. He sensed the change in my heart, and we would talk about things, about what he was experiencing, and about the fears he was having. Everything started to change from that time on as far as our relationship. It didn't mean that he could change himself, but it meant that I could be there to help him and support him.

When we were going through these troubles, a gentleman from church headquarters in Salt Lake City came to talk to our stake about temples. He told us that we don't use the power of the temple to our benefit enough. It's important to go to the temple with a broken heart and a contrite spirit, fasting and truly yearning and desiring for what you want. When you walk into the temple, you pray for what you desire and throughout the temple ceremonies you carry this deep, deep concern and prayer in your heart. You petition your Heavenly Father every second that you can.

My husband and I decided that this was what we needed to do to help our son. We needed to call down

The Battle Maidens of the Lord

the powers of heaven in the temple to help us. So that is what we did. It seemed like afterwards there wasn't any huge experience. It was a series of things that happened. The first thing we started noticing was that our son's attitude was changing. Derek had a desire to change, and started driving himself over to a town forty miles away to a drug abuse recovery program for youth.

Then we decided that we would like him to go to a wilderness program where you are taught to love yourself. We felt that it would be a good program for him, but he never would say that he would go. When it came time to put in the papers, he didn't know what to say to me.

"Well son, let me tell you why I want you to go. All of my life I have loved nature and spent a lot of time walking in the mountains and hiking and climbing. Each time I'm alone with nature, I've been able to feel my Heavenly Father love me and express His love for me. That is what I want for you. I want you to be able to feel your Heavenly Father carry you and tell you that He loves you, that you are a worthwhile being and that you are important," I said.

He confessed that the reason that he didn't want to go was because of the expense. It was expensive. Derek already felt so guilty for all the trouble he had caused us. But he ended up going, and it was a wonderful experience for him.

While our Derek was gone, we had a big Pioneer Day celebration. That year my husband was in charge of the celebration and had invited a prominent native son to be the grand marshal in the parade. We offered to have a reunion for the family of this good man to entice him to come. All their family came, and it was a wonderful experience. We developed an endearing relationship with this family.

When Derek came home, he was ready to enter his senior year of high school. He kept telling me that he felt like he needed to leave, that he couldn't stay here. I was really selfish and didn't want to lose him.

"Oh, I think you would be such a good example. Not everyone can send their child to a program like you've been to. You've learned so much," I said.

His dad also was trying to tell me that he felt like our son needed to leave. One day I was impressed to call the wife of the family who had had the reunion at our home and ask her if our son could go and stay with them.

"I was just standing in this room and wondering if I might finally be able to turn it into the office that I've always wanted. I was wondering if the Lord was going to send me someone this year or not. I guess I have my answer now," she said.

So our son went to stay far away. This family has a son Derek's age. At midnight he and his friends met our boy at the airport and spent the whole night on the beach with him. Derek felt like he was home. It was a miracle. To this day each of those boys have remained close friends. Derek developed strength and went on a mission to teach the gospel of Jesus Christ to others. Later he was married in the temple.

The Battle Maidens of the Lord

As we look back, we can see all these little steps that led to the miracle. We felt like it was because of the powers of the temple and the powers of the priesthood that he was able to have these wonderful blessings in his life. He is a wonderful, loving young man and a great gift to us.

The Lord will give us answers to our prayers. He will send the comforter to give us peace and to calm our troubled hearts. He listens and knows what is best for us all. Fortunately, He will share his wisdom if His children will ask, then listen. Many things will go better than we ever imagined or hoped for. That is not to say that He will force someone or take away agency. That is one thing it does no good to ask for. However, He will lead and guide and give help along the way. If asked, Heavenly Father will tell us what to pray for. Knowing what to pray for is important. It makes the difference between floundering around in prayers and praying with a focused purpose.

Other great allies in the battle against evil are our family, friends and church leaders. Families can be a great blessing in times of trial. When God, priesthood power, parents, and children work together, great things can be accomplished. Husbands, fathers and other priesthood leaders are some of our greatest allies. The next two stories are those of a father and mother working together as allies with their Heavenly Father to save their son from Satan's power. The following is the father's experience.

Jaqueline Ethington
THE JOURNEY BACK

When our son was seventeen years old, his mother found marijuana in his pockets while doing the laundry. He had become addicted. Being self-employed, I shut down the business for however long it was going to take to help our son. I determined that I would take him on a trip away from where we lived and away from friends, away from everything. It had to be long enough that whatever drugs he may have in his system would wear off. At which point I hoped I could reason with the young man himself and not be talking to the effects that the drugs might be having on him. He needed to have the ability to think clearly and to reason.

The first few days of that trip were an absolute nightmare. It was beyond anything that I had ever experienced in my life. This was a young man completely out of control, one I didn't know or recognize. Of course, I was dealing with the effects of drug withdrawal.

At some point while in a motel room, he determined he was going to run away. Who knows where he would have gone in a strange city, knowing no one, having no money or means. He did leave, and I had to bring him back to the room. I put my bed right up against the door so there was no way out. After a while of loud protest, he went to sleep. I slipped out of my bed and began to pray. It was not one of the kinds of prayers that I was used to saying, where you do your duty and in a minute or two you are up and ready to go to bed. This prayer went on for hours and hours. In the early morning, the answer came to take this young man to the

The Battle Maidens of the Lord

home of my brother. He was a righteous member of the church and was raising a fine family. There were several girls in my brother's family about my son's age. I didn't know why, but I did know that was what I needed to do.

The next morning I called my brother, and we headed for his place. It was summertime, and he was home doing a remodeling project on his house. We worked alongside him and his family. The influence of those young, righteous ladies on my son was dramatic. All of the rebelliousness and all of the anger was gone. He was back to the person I had always known and loved.

We stayed there a couple of nights. I especially remember one of those nights. We were sleeping in the front bedroom that they had given up for us, and I was praying again. The answer that came was completely surprising to me. Although I had been a good member of the church all of my life and had served a mission, I had discounted the real power of Satan. I had not thought about that. I had thought about God and Christ and Joseph Smith and all the wonderful and positive things the gospel teaches. I had never considered the real and present power that Satan has in this life.

It became clear to me that my son had gotten in over his head because of the things he had chosen to do. Satan wanted him. The counter balancing power of the Holy Ghost was not there to make the playing field level. When I realized this, it was an absolute revelation to me. I knew that because of the overwhelming power of Satan, my son was not in a position to overcome Satan's hold on him by himself. I began to pray. As I did this, I felt an absolutely overwhelming coldness come into the room. It was a summer night, and we had the windows open because it was so hot, but I was as cold as if I had been kneeling there in the middle of a snowstorm. I was afraid, very afraid, but I prayed.

I asked the Lord to intervene in my son's behalf. I asked Him to put a shield of protection around him, to send guardian angels. I asked that He would not allow Satan to have such terrible power over him. I felt instinctively that it was not right that I should ask that he would not have any temptation or that Satan would not have any power in his life. That was the whole purpose for our being here upon the earth, to have that opposition. I just wanted him to have a level playing field, to have only the normal temptations of a person his age. If he so desired and could be brought to that point, I prayed that he would have the power within himself to turn his life around. He needed protection until such time as he could deserve the Holy Ghost to be with him to protect him.

It took a while, and he did continue to struggle, but that was the low point. He gradually turned his life around and went on a mission. Later, he was married in the temple to a beautiful and righteous young lady.

I look back on that experience as the turning point in our son's life. It was something he had to do. I couldn't do it for him. But I do know that the power of the priesthood was able to reach into the jaws of hell and bless, to give a chance to a young man who was heading in the wrong direction. Through his own desires, hard work, and effort, he repented of his sins. Because the Lord had his hand there and answered my prayers and the prayers of his mother, our beloved son changed his life. I'll be eternally grateful for Heavenly Father's willingness to hear and answer the prayers of parents who were trying to save their posterity.

The young man's mother's experience was different.

I HAVE A PLACE FOR YOU

For his twelfth birthday, my son wanted to travel to Salt Lake City to go to the semi-annual conference of the Church of Jesus Christ of Latter-day Saints. His father and I and our children made the long trip to Utah. The appointed day came, and we waited outside in the rain at the end of a long line to get into the tabernacle. Conference had just started, and it didn't look like there was any chance of getting in. Then an usher stuck his head out of the back door.

"You just bring those children in here out of the rain. I have a place for you," he said.

Years later when the birthday child had his missionary farewell, one of those talks heard at that conference was used as the basis for a fine sermon.

Between the time he was thirteen and his mission farewell, he made friends with some young people who were misguided. He and his friends were not making good choices at the time. Our son didn't keep the word of wisdom, but he read the Book of Mormon every day because the prophet had told him to.

37

Jaqueline Ethington

His father and I were frantic. We prayed a lot,
read scriptures, tried to be good examples, and made
many mistakes. When our son was seventeen, he went
away on a trip with his father. When he returned, things
began to improve. But being a typical mom, I wanted
faster results. I asked the Lord for what I should be
praying. He told me an important thing to pray for, and I
did it. But today I cannot remember what it was.

My son had a sure testimony of the gospel and
knew that Jesus was the Christ. He even knew what his
mission here on the earth was to be. I felt that, like
Jonah, one of the things our son was doing was running
from that mission. So I prayed that a whale would
swallow him. I felt that three days in the belly of a whale
would just about do it. While he was away at college, the
whale showed up at the door.

Our son was spending the evening at a party in
the apartment of friends. Someone invited a group of
drunken strangers in to join the fun. On spotting my
son, they took an instant dislike to him. As a group, they
picked him up and proceeded to the third floor balcony
determined to throw him over. Fear flooded the hapless
victim as death opened its jaws three floors below.

A determined friend finally persuaded the group
not to carry out their plans. Upon being released, my son
left the party filled with anger toward the drunks.

"I hate those people. I'm glad I will never be like
them," he said in his heart.

And then it struck him that he was becoming
exactly like them. He was so startled when he came to

The Battle Maidens of the Lord

that realization that he began to take a good look at himself. The next day was Sunday, and he went to church as usual. Sitting there in sacrament meeting he felt the Holy Ghost and the spirits of his future children strongly encouraging him to live righteously. He made up his mind to change for good. And he did.

Each person involved in the same situation will have a different experience. These differing points of view of the same circumstance give an added dimension to the help that is requested from God. Consequently, multifaceted help comes. A rich mixture of blessings and assistance begins to descend from heaven.

The Lord loves all of His children. He will bless them and give them experiences designed to bring them to him, even if there is no one to pray for them. Many times there is only one person to pray for one of God's lost sheep. If that person is the lone supplicant at the throne of God, they should certainly not be discouraged. He will hear them. Sometimes people will use their agency to refuse to listen to the Lord calling to them. That certainly does happen. Nevertheless, Those who pray for the wayward should not give up praying. Eternity is a long time.

There are great allies in the battles against evil. If we will enlist our families and ask for help from God, we Battle Maidens do not have to fight our battles alone. Each parent in these stories sought to reach and teach their children in a different way. There is really no right way to do things. However, one thing that these parents

39

all had in common is that they all sought the Lord for help through prayer. These prayers were answered in different ways because God knows what will help His various children. We need to seek the powers of heaven in the temple. We need to ask what we should be praying for, then pray and listen to the promptings of the Holy Ghost. Christ, the captain or our salvation, experienced earth life and all of its pitfalls. He understands our circumstances and is ready and infinitely capable of aiding us.

Chapter 5

Christ, the Captain of our Salvation

For I have given you an example, that ye should do as I have done...
John 13:15[24]

Christ gave us the example of how to resist temptation. Satan has tried to put a modern face on sin by calling it the new morality. However, the new morality is just plain, old-fashioned sin. And temptation can be defeated by the successful methods used throughout the ages. Let's just take a good look at what Christ did when He was tempted.

After Jesus was baptized by John the Baptist when he was about thirty years of age, He went into the wilderness. There He fasted for forty days and communed with His Father in heaven. When He returned to civilization, hungry, the devil thought that it would be the perfect time to tempt Him. Weak with hunger as he supposed Christ to be, the devil sneered, *...If you be the Son of God, command that these stones be made bread.*[25] Satan tried to appeal to the weakness of His body. Today Satan might appeal to a desire for liquor, cigarettes, drugs, or illicit passions. Something as seemingly

41

innocent as food certainly can still work as a temptation. Christ resisted this temptation *and informed him that Man shall not live by bread alone, but by every word that proceedeth out of the mouth of God.*[26] His body may have been weakened, but His Spirit had been strengthened.

Jesus knew the scriptures and was able to use them to His benefit. This is one reason that we have been admonished to read the scriptures daily. We may not be able to quote them, but we can certainly remember God's messages and bring them to mind. It is a good idea to always keep our spirits in tune with the Holy Ghost and in good fighting order. We never know when we will have to do battle against temptation and evil.

Then the devil took Jesus to the top of the temple *and saith unto him, If thou be the Son of God, cast thyself down: for it is written, He shall give his angels charge concerning thee: and in their hands they shall bear thee up, lest at any time thou dash thy foot against a stone.*[27] The temptation to save Himself would have appeal to Christ's vanity. If He had been vain, Christ could have say, "Look at me. Aren't I great? I can float. Hey, look at me." Once again the devil used the sneering "if."

Christ didn't doubt who He was. He was a member of the Godhead. Women shouldn't doubt who they are either. We are children of God with a royal heritage. When we are baptized, we have the privilege of having the Holy Ghost, a member of the Godhead, as a constant companion. No "if" should ever be daunting to the soul anchored in Christ. Sometimes our anchors tend to get pulled and dragged a little across the bottom of the

The Battle Maidens of the Lord

sea. In that case, just a desire to believe and a hope that the gospel is true will bring blessings from God, and He will strengthen and help His children walk away from evil.

After this temptation, *Jesus said unto him, It is written again, Thou shalt not tempt the Lord thy God.*[28]

It is indeed not a good idea to tempt the Lord to perform miracles to amaze and satisfy the lust for notoriety. In an incident from the Book of Mormon, Korihor learned this painful lesson. Even though the prophet Alma had warned him not to ask for a sign, he asked anyway.

Now Korihor, in his best political double speak, said this: *I do not deny the existence of a God, but I do not believe that there is a God; and I say also, that ye do not know that there is a God; and except ye show me a sign, I will not believe.*[29] Then Alma gave him his sign from God. Korihor was struck dumb and could speak no more. He learned his lesson too late.

The devil had a third try at tempting Christ. *Again, the devil taketh him up into an exceeding high mountain, and sheweth him all the kingdoms of the world, and the glory of them; and said unto him, All these things will I give thee, if thou wilt fall down and worship me.*[30] This was an appeal to the love for power and fame to which the natural man frequently falls prey. Since Christ had created the earth, the heavens and all that are in them, they belonged to Him anyway. But He needed to be tempted in all things, as is the human family.

Power, fame and worldly glory are great temptations to many in the world. One has only to read

43

the newspapers to see how yielding to this can bring a moral breakdown. This human weakness is pointed out in latter-day revelation. *We have learned by sad experience that it is the nature and disposition of almost all men, as soon as they get a little authority, as they suppose, they will immediately begin to exercise unrighteous dominion.*[31]

Satan wanted to be worshiped as the Christ, just as he wanted to be named the Christ in the pre-mortal world. Before the flood when only Noah and his family were saved, Satan came to the children of Adam telling them not to believe the prophet Adam's teachings. The Apostle Paul says, "*... for Satan himself is transformed into an angel of light.*[32] Moses tells us, *And Satan came among them* (the children of Adam and Eve), *saying: I am also a son of God; and he commanded them, saying: Believe it not; and they believed it not, and they loved Satan more than God. And men began from that time forth to be carnal, sensual, and devilish.*[33] This had disastrous results. The world became so wicked that all but a few souls were destroyed in the flood because of wickedness. The prophet Enoch saw Satan's glee at his handiwork. *And he beheld Satan; and he had a great chain in his hand, and it veiled the whole face of the earth with darkness; and he looked up and laughed, and his angels rejoiced.*[34] Yes indeed, Satan wanted Christ to worship him. He wanted to scoop up Christ's position as a god.

When the last temptation was over, *Then saith Jesus unto him, Get thee hence, Satan: for it is written Thou shalt worship the Lord thy God, and him only shalt thou serve.*[35] There it is. When Satan comes tempting, he must be told to leave. Say, "Get thee hence, Satan." This is done in the name of Jesus Christ. He can be ignored and no heed paid to him. This is what Christ did. *He suffered temptations but gave no heed unto them.*[36] Christ tells us to watch and pray that we enter not into temptation.[37] He also gives us comfort in our struggles to overcome temptation when He tells us that with the temptation, He will provide us with a means of escape.[38] The Lord knows how to deliver His righteous children from temptation.[39] One other thing is needful. The Lord only must be served, not Satan.

If we are in a place that is tempting by its nature, we can say to our feet, "Let's go feet and get out of this bad place." Leave any place where temptation and evil are present. Get up and go. It is better to not go to such a place, but sometimes the righteous will find themselves surrounded by evil unexpectedly.

President David O. McKay said this, "Your weakest point will be the point at which the Devil tries to tempt you, and if you have made it weak before you have undertaken to serve the Lord, he will add to that weakness. Resist him and you will gain in strength. He will tempt you in another point. Resist him and he becomes weaker and you become stronger, until you can say, no matter what your surroundings may be, 'Get thee behind me, Satan: for it is written, Thou shalt worship the Lord thy God, and him only shalt thou serve."[40]

After these three temptations, *Then the devil leaveth him, and, behold, angels came and ministered unto him.*[41] Every time that evil is resisted, we become stronger. The Holy Ghost will comfort and aid us. Angels also minister

45

unto us. These angels may not be seen, but at times their presence can be felt. But felt or not, the Lord has promised the righteous heavenly help. *...I will go before your face. I will be on your right hand and on your left, and my Spirit shall be in your hearts, and mine angels round about you, to bear you up.*[42]

Christ is indeed our great exemplar in all things, including the overcoming of the temptations of Satan and his minions. We can look to the ways that Christ handled Satan during the devil's big push at tempting Him. Christ didn't belittle or treat Satan disrespectfully, but simply didn't heed the temptation and in the end commanded him to leave. We have been given the same power. We can do this. We can work hard at paying no heed to Satan's temptations, and if it is needful, we can command him to leave in the name of Jesus Christ. We are here on the earth to do the will of the Lord and to prove ourselves. It will be a struggle, but it is important that we are here fighting the good fight.

Chapter 6

Boots on the Ground

And he said unto me:
Behold, the virgin whom thou seest
Is the mother of the Son of God,
after the manner of the flesh.
1 Nephi 11:18[43]

God needs his daughters to be here on the ground in the battlefield of life to teach His children the gospel, to help them gain a testimony and great faith. Jesus needed Mary to love Him, protect Him, and teach Him just as He needed His Heavenly Father and Joseph. Mary had to be there personally engaged in the battle for her son. She needed to be there with her boots on the ground to protect Him while He was young.

Satan stalked around the perimeter of her home like a wolf snarling at the gate, hoping for an opportunity to get in. Mary would keep Satan at bay by taking up the stick of righteousness and giving him a good, sharp rap on the nose. Acts of kindness, service, love, and obedience to God's commandments ensure that Satan cannot overpower us. These are the whacking sticks that keep Satan away.

It is doubtful that Mary was a delicate, timid, little thing. She was a strong woman who could be engaging to

Jaqueline Ethington

her neighbors, but they probably didn't miss the fact that she was not one to be trifled with. She was, after all, one of the greatest and most valiant spirits of heaven, a true Battle Maiden of the Lord. Could the Son of God be entrusted to anyone less?

For he shall give his angels charge over thee, to keep thee in all thy ways. They shall bear thee up in their hands, lest thou dash thy foot against a stone.[44] Doesn't that sound like a mother? Mary was one of the angels assigned to have charge over Jesus Christ, Lord of heaven and earth. She carried her little son many times when his steps were faltering, lest he dash his foot against a stone.

Like Mary, there were many men and women in the pre-mortal world prepared for special missions on earth as the prophet Joseph F. Smith saw in vision. *I observed that they (the latter-day prophets) were also among the noble and great ones who were chosen in the beginning to be rulers in the Church of God. Even before they were born, they, with many others, received their first lessons in the world of spirits and were prepared to come forth in the due time of the Lord to labor in his vineyard for the salvation of the souls of men.*[45]

Mary was one of those chosen in the beginning to do the work of God, to bear His son. She was also prepared to come forth in the due time of the Lord.

Her life was difficult. She had to flee the land of her birth and, at times, endure persecution from her neighbors and family. When these kinds of things happened, Mary would go to a quiet place and ponder the events of Christ's birth in her heart. She would remember the angel, Gabriel, his message to her, and her consent to do the will of the Lord. Mary would recall her visit to her cousin Elizabeth. She would picture the shepherds coming in happy reverence to see the new baby, Jesus, and would remember their stories of angels singing and glory streaming from on high. Memories of wise men from the East, with their awe and respect, would ease her troubled mind. Her true self would come bubbling to the top once again.

Can you see Mary? Her face and hands are browned by the sun. Her cheerful, happy personality shines through in her smile. She sings a little song as she holds a baby on one hip and throws feed from her apron pocket to the chickens. Running around her feet, scattering the flock, are the rest of her little ones who are happy to be in her presence. As she milks the goats, she teaches little Jesus about Adam naming the animals. She is anxious to teach him and her other children all the stories of the prophets and the scriptures.

Mary seldom travels far from home and family. On market day, a group of active little children follows her down the road. One chases a butterfly, and one catches a frog. When the little group finally returns home, Mary collapses on a cushion, grateful to be there. Her life was not so very much different from most of the world's women, and in many respects neither was her mission.

God has a work for His army of daughters to do here upon the earth. He needs a great army with their boots on the ground, fighting the good fight. He is sending his most valiant spirits to earth now, spirits he has saved for millennia to come here at this time. That means a mother's job is vital since these children are the key that turns in the lock that opens the door to the coming of Christ. Satan will try to snatch them away. Get the whacking stick out and be ready to smack him on the snout. Let righteous works keep him away. Teach these precious children the gospel well, go to the temple often, serve in wards and stakes, listen for the Holy Ghost, and obey His instructions immediately. Watch over that little flock of children like a hawk. *The glory of God is intelligence, or, in other words, light and truth. Light and truth forsake that evil one.... And that wicked one cometh and taketh away light and truth, through disobedience, from the children of men, and because of the traditions of their fathers. But I have commanded you to bring up your children in light and truth.*[46]

There are many missions for the great Battle Maidens of the Lord to perform. In the account written by Helaman in <u>The Book of Mormon,</u> we learn about a group of young warriors and their Lamanite mothers who had their boots on the ground. This is what Helaman had to say. *Yea, they had been taught by their mothers, that if they did not doubt, God would deliver them. And they rehearsed unto me the words of their mothers, saying: we do not doubt our mothers knew it.*[47] In a long and bloody war where many were killed, these faithful young men, who had been taught by their mothers not to doubt God, all came home alive.

A portion of the Lord's spiritual warriors of today, missionaries, need to spread over the whole earth. We

The Battle Maidens of the Lord
need to be like the mothers of the young soldiers of
Helaman. We need to teach our children to join in
God's army and fight the good fight. God needs boots on
the ground. That missionary army is not nearly big
enough. The following is a missionary story of a convert
and his wife who set their hearts on God. They walked
through life scattering seeds of testimony that eventually
spread throughout the earth and bloomed in generations
that they never lived to see.

HOW MISS LUCINDA RECEIVED THE
GOSPEL
"In the winter of 1844, I, James Richey, was
working for Mr. Henson six miles from our home in
Mississippi. When I came home on Saturday night, the
whole neighborhood was excited. The Mormons had
come to preach. They would be preaching again on the
next Sunday, and I was determined to hear them. I had
heard preachers of various religions speak before and
found a lack in my bosom from hearing them. They
didn't follow the teachings of Christ as I had understood
them from reading the <u>Bible</u>. When the day came, I sat
myself down in front of the speaker and listened to him
tell of the authenticity of the <u>Book of Mormon</u> and the
restoration of the Gospel of Christ. There was a spirit
and power there that I had never before seen manifest.
"I soon discovered that Mormons were unpopular.
Not wanting to give up my good name with the world, I
studied the <u>Bible</u> hoping to prove them wrong. But the
more I read, the more I came to believe it was true. The

void in my breast was filled. I was baptized in a beautiful stream of water by Benjamin L. Cluff and was confirmed by the laying on of hands to receive the gift of the Holy Ghost.

"That night as I lay contemplating the principles of the Gospel, all at once the Holy Spirit came upon me, and I was filled with joy unspeakable and was full of glory. I could feel it from the crown of my head to the soles of my feet. I very soon awakened all that were in the house and bore a strong testimony to them in regards to the truth of the Gospel as restored through the Prophet Joseph Smith, in consequence of which my Father and brother, Benjamin, went and were baptized the next morning."

James was soon made an Elder, and in company with Brother Cluff and others, he proceeded to carry the good news to first his father's family and then his mother's. While teaching the gospel, James heard disparaging things about the Prophet Joseph and Nauvoo. He immediately made the long trip north to Nauvoo in the state of Illinois and found the gossip to be false. When he first arrived, he met the Prophet Joseph and spent the night in the Mansion House with his family.

After two weeks in Nauvoo, James returned to the South in company with others, preaching the everlasting gospel as he went. He brought the restored gospel to the Mangum, Adair, and Price families among others. He, his family, and the saints from the South moved to Nauvoo. In Nauvoo James married Miss Lucinda Mangum, his most beloved convert. They stayed faithful all through

The Battle Maidens of the Lord

their lives and have thousands of faithful decedents. Many of these children and grandchildren, down six and seven generations at this time, have also been great missionaries and have searched the earth for the elect of God. (Taken from the Journal of James Richey)

After joining the church, Lucinda and James firmly planted their boots in the gospel sod and raised a family tutored in faith, service, and obedience to the laws of God.

And if it so be that you should labor all your days in crying repentance unto this people, and bring save it be one soul unto me, how great shall be your joy with him in the kingdom of my Father! And now, if your joy will be great with one soul that you have brought unto me into the kingdom of my Father, how great will be your joy if you should bring many souls unto me.[48]

In addition to preparation for missionary work, we need to be preparing for the Zion which God has promised us will come in these last days. God needs boots on the ground to bring about the promised Zion. Now how does one go about establishing Zion? We, with our husbands, have the responsibility to raise up a Zion family. Looking at the history of the earth, we might think that it is a nearly impossible task. At any other time that would probably be right. But this time things are different. God is sending a Zion people to the earth. *Therefore, verily, thus saith the Lord, let Zion rejoice, for this is Zion—THE PURE IN HEART; therefore, let Zion rejoice.*[49] He is sending a people capable of being pure in heart. It is our job to bring up that righteous generation. We are able to do it, too~for we are also a Zion generation.

Jaqueline Ethington

Zion has several meanings, but the only one considered here will be the Zion of the pure in heart. President Spencer W. Kimball gave several attributes to work on in order to bring Zion into the hearts of the people. He said that we must become unselfish, then we must become united and work harmoniously with each other. He added that we needed to offer up a willing heart and humble spirit to the Lord and do what he requires of us. And finally we must keep our temple covenants and follow the promptings of the Holy Ghost.[50]

Where do we learn to do all these excellent things? We learn to do them in our homes. Families diligently teach the gospel of Christ and follow the principles taught by their church leaders. "The Family: A Proclamation to the World" is a wonderful guide from church leaders and the Lord. It is important to note that the church is designed to assist the family in teaching our children, not the other way around.

Most young parents are doing an excellent job of teaching from the scriptures and following the promptings of the Holy Ghost. After all, they are a chosen generation. Once in a while, it is the children who are the strong ones, and they teach their parents correct principles. It works out well if they have teachable parents.

Zion cannot be built up unless it is by the principles of the law of the celestial kingdom.[51] The saints are living this law more and more frequently. Here are some recent examples of the celestial law in action.

The Battle Maidens of the Lord

After primary activity day, eight-year-old Sally carefully put her frosted valentine cookies into a paper bag. She took them home to her younger brothers and sisters.

When the Bishop asked his ward members if there were any who could help those out of work find jobs, two men immediately came forward. One offered to help any qualified individual through the process of applying and interviewing for a job at the large company where he worked. Another man knew of two openings for persons with advanced computer skills. He was anxious to find qualified people.

A recently retired couple went out on a spring day to work in their garden. Side by side they dug and weeded and prepared the ground. No unhelpful suggestions crossed the space between them. Birds sang, the air was fresh, and there was a feeling of great peace. They were sharing a Zion experience.

The Relief Society President, Bunny Jones, learned that Sister Dawn in her ward had an important meeting to attend. Sister Dawn's husband had lost his job, and there was very little money even for necessities. Because of their tight budget, she did not have anything appropriate to wear. Bunny brought Sister Dawn to her home where they looked through her large stash of dressmaking fabric. After Sister Dawn selected fabric and a pattern, Bunny, an excellent seamstress, proceeded to sew a new outfit for Sister Dawn. Sister Dawn went to her meeting with confidence, partly because she felt comfortable in her appearance.

Jaqueline Ethington

When Tess Jakes' daughter became engaged to be married in the temple to a fine young man, she was plunged into happiness to have such a wonderful blessing come to her family. It was the first Jakes temple marriage in twenty-seven years. Peggy came up to her after church and said, "Tess, I rejoice with you at the marriage of your daughter. I am so happy for you. What a wonderful thing this is." Tess's heart filled with love for Peggy as they rejoiced together.

Zion experiences are the simple, everyday things that we do with love and patience. They are not big exercises executed with fanfare and notoriety. For example, programs of the church that are implemented to serve others, such as the Relief Society, the employment program and the welfare program, quietly lead us in becoming a Zion people. As Satan increases in power, these types of Zion activities will become more and more important.

We are actually capable of bringing Zion to earth in small areas right now. A home that is harmonious and filled with love is a bit of Zion. It may last for only a short time or for years. Perhaps we have been to Zion. It doesn't happen until we have learned to follow the teachings of Christ. Even then it is kind of an on and off thing. But every once in a while, a shining Zion can be seen peeking through the clouds even though this is the day of Satan's power

The day speedily cometh; the hour is not yet, but is nigh at hand, when peace shall be taken from the earth, and the devil shall have power over his own dominion.[52] This prophesy

56

The Battle Maidens of the Lord
from the Lord was written in 1831. In the January, 1991, *Ensign*, President Ezra Taft Benson wrote that this was being fulfilled. "Satan, in undiminished fury, is displaying power over 'his own dominion'—the earth." He further went on to say that evil influences had never been greater and that listening to the Holy Ghost and our priesthood leaders was the only sure path to safety.[53]

As time has passed, Satan's influence has become even greater. It is easy to see that it is important that the church members become a Zion people. We have to help each other and our neighbors and put each other's concerns on the same level as our own. There is great protection in living the celestial law. The people of God have to put themselves in a position to receive the help of God. Pray for the establishment of Zion. Satan will do all in his power to stop it, but he won't succeed.

Nephi prophesied that the Saints of this day would have the power of God because of their efforts to be a righteous people, a Zion people. *And it came to pass that I, Nephi, beheld the power of the Lamb of God, that it descended upon the saints of the church of the Lamb, and upon the covenant people of the Lord, who were scattered upon all the face of the earth; and they were armed with righteousness and with the power of God in great glory.*[54]

The Lord needs His Battle Maidens with their boots on the ground to be busily engaged in the work of the kingdom here on the earth. These great women are not just those who are mothers but also teachers, primary workers and, young women's leaders and all who work in the Kingdom of God. The Lord also needs the

57

priesthood contingency to be hard at work in this important task. There is much to be done in raising a righteous generation who are prepared to take the gospel to the whole earth, that Zion might be established, and the earth prepared for the second coming of Christ in glory.

Chapter 7

Pray for a Brave Heart

I have spoken unto you
That in me ye might have peace.
In the world ye shall have tribulation:
But be of good cheer; I have overcome the world.
John 16:33[55]

Because the people of the latter days are among the great and valiant ones, they will have serious trials and temptations in this life. It seems to follow that the stronger the spirit of an individual, the greater his or her trials will be. But the women of today knew what their missions and situations would be on earth and agreed to them before they came. The Battle Maidens knew this because of the principle of foreordination in the pre-mortal world. One cannot agree to do something if she doesn't know what it is. "These pre-mortal appointments, made "'according to the foreknowledge of God the Father' (1 Pet. 1:2) simply designated certain individuals to perform missions which the Lord in his wisdom knew they had the talents and capacities to do...In all this there is not the slightest hint of compulsion; persons foreordained to fill special missions in mortality are as abundantly endowed with free agency as are any other persons."[56]

Jaqueline Ethington

The spirit children of God rightly thought that they could complete these tasks successfully. These spirits, now clothed in mortal bodies, are here to fight against unrighteous dominion and evil on the earth. *Be sober, be vigilant; because your adversary the devil, as a roaring lion, walketh about, seeking whom he may devour.*[57] Even though we will have considerable opposition from those inspired by the devil, we will succeed in our missions because we have the companionship of the Holy Ghost and the Light of Christ to protect, to help, and to guide us.

We knew that the times in which we were destined to live would be filled with peril, and that we would be stalked by the evil one. However, we also understood that God knew us well and had saved us for this day. Since God thought that we could handle this generation that is saturated with evil, who are we to question His judgment? He warned us about what we would have to face. *For we wrestle not against flesh and blood, but against principalities, against powers, against the rulers of the darkness of this world, against spiritual wickedness in high places.*[58] God warned us and then sent us forth to accomplish His will.

God also gave us a way to know what we face and be able to make correct judgments about what we see going on around us. *For behold, the Spirit of Christ is given to every man, that he may know good from evil; wherefore, I show unto you the way to judge; for every thing which inviteth to do good, and to persuade to believe in Christ, is sent forth by the power and gift of Christ; wherefore; ye may know with a perfect*

60

The Battle Maidens of the Lord

knowledge it is of God. But whatsoever thing persuadeth men to do evil, and believe not in Christ, and deny him, and serve not God, then ye may know with a perfect knowledge it is of the devil; for after this manner doth the devil work, for he persuadeth no man to do good, no, not one; neither do his angels; neither do they who subject themselves unto him.[59] And so we are perfectly capable of knowing good from evil for the Lord has given us a blueprint to follow.

From time to time things are going to be difficult, but that is the nature of life. If life were always pleasant and lovely, it wouldn't be a test of our willingness to obey God. Sometimes we will need to stand up in a public forum for the principles that we hold dear. Together many of the citizens of the world will be bravely fighting to preserve the traditional values of civilized society. Those of us fighting on the Lord's side showed our bravery in the pre-mortal world. Courage is our birthright. Nevertheless, pray for a brave heart. In the following story, Danielle prayed mightily for a brave heart.

I CROSSED THE LINE

I've never liked being pushed around and threatened. Once, when I was teaching school in a big city, there was a drive to have all the teachers join the teacher's union. I thought about some of the good things that unions do and was seriously considering joining.

While passing through the hall at school one morning, an English teacher stopped me and threatened me. He informed me that I had better join the union or bad things would happen to me. I informed him that I

61

had been seriously considering joining, but that now I would never join an organization that used threats and intimidation.

Shortly after this incident, the union went on strike. I was determined not to be intimidated, and I decided to cross the picket line. On the morning of the strike, I walked toward the line of union picketers. As I approached the line, the picketers threw pennies at me and called me names. But I crossed the line and went to work. As I said, I don't like to be threatened.

At times, women personally have to stand on the battle lines against the philosophy of the world and defend their position as Christians. It takes courage, steadfastness, and faith. Elizabeth, in the following story, is a person who exhibited that courage, steadfastness, and faith in dealing with her trials in life.

HOME AT LAST

When we lived in the city, my husband, a building contractor, built our final home, the one we were going to live in the rest of our lives. We had neighbors we loved, seven children, and a good life. Then the interest rate on our home loan changed. It was right when the bottom fell out of the housing market.

A lot of people were affected by the market downturn. A man down the street lost his home and moved to another city three hundred miles away. It turned out well, however, because he started a successful business and later became the Stake President. Also, his wife got her college degree.

The Battle Maidens of the Lord

However, the financial situation was difficult for my husband. He worked so hard, but we could not keep up the payments on our house. He got some jobs in his hometown, two hundred miles away, so he would work there during the week and live with his widowed mother, Ellen. Then he would come home on the weekends. I tried to help financially by doing some babysitting.

We thought we might have to move to my husband's hometown, a small and remote place, so my husband took our two older girls there to high school the last three months of the school year. They wanted to try out for cheer leading. The three of them would drive up for school and work during the week, and I would stay home with the younger children. My daughters did succeed in making the cheer squad. At this time, our oldest son was getting ready to go on his mission.

We tried to sell our home, but it just wouldn't sell so I called the bank and told them that we couldn't make the payments on our house. The bank was very nice and told us not to worry. They would take the house back.

When you own your own business, your taxes are high, and we couldn't pay. The government learned that we were going to turn our house back to the bank. Subsequently, the IRS slapped a lean on the house, and the bank couldn't take it back. That meant bankruptcy.

I'll never forget the last night we spent in our home. It was hot. Our son had just left on his mission, and we had sold everything we owned except our beds. As we left the next morning, I looked back at our house, and there was a heavy weight on my heart.

Jaqueline Ethington

"It's O.K. I'll be all right. This is an adventure with six kids," I said to myself.

It kind of was an adventure, a long adventure. We packed up everything and went to a small town with no job. We lived in a little two-bedroom apartment on the same grounds as my mother-in-law, Ellen. Some of the kids slept in her house, and some slept where we were. At night I'd go and tuck them in bed at the big house and then go back to our apartment. When the children would become afraid at night during a thunderstorm, they would run out in the rain and come and jump in bed with us. Sometimes things would get bad, and I would feel sorry for myself. What saved me was prayer and scriptures, not just my prayers, but also family prayers and scripture study. We have lots of memories.

When we moved in with my husband's mother, she encouraged us to get our education.

"I'm here to take care of your children. This is your chance," Ellen said. So we went to school and got our college degrees.

When we first got to town, the seminary teacher came to me and said, "I don't know why, but I'm impressed to ask you to be a seminary teacher." I gladly agreed and taught two or three days a week. They paid me. I worked hard and got my commercial driver's license and drove a school bus to earn extra money while we were in school. My husband built on the side, and it worked out. It was a struggle, of course. We didn't have much money, but we didn't have any bills either. Eventually we got our college degrees and were hired as teachers at the school. Now I've got a master's degree.

After twenty years, I'm still living with Ellen. It is still her furniture. The pots and pans are hers, but now I don't know any different. It has been nothing but good because she is a wonderful person. She is very loving with her grandchildren and with us, too. When I look back, it was hard, but we had to get through it. If I think about our home and trials we have gone through, I can get teary-eyed. I won't do that. That was the past, and it is over now. Ellen ended up giving us her home, and it has worked out. It is good. We are doing fine.

Instead of moaning about how things used to be and how they ought to have been, Elizabeth looked ahead. She walked with courage into a world that she didn't choose and made the best of it. In time, the new world she had entered became her world, and she commanded an important place in that world because of her resilient and kind nature.

There are other resilient people who can laugh in the face of persecution. Olivia is just such a person.

GUESS WHAT

Before I married, I worked as an intern for an international company, and I had several friends from other countries. There was one woman in particular, Tatty, with whom I had had several conversations about Christ and my spiritual beliefs. She knew that I was a virgin and that was remarkable to her. It was hard for her

Jaqueline Ethington

to believe anyone actually practiced chastity. Her marriage was an open marriage. She and her husband apparently didn't value faithfulness.

Our company invited all the interns and others out to eat with the executives one Friday. This dinner was to be followed by a night at the theater. We were all seated around a large table in an elegant restaurant when in a loud voice Tatty made a big announcement.

"Guess what! Olivia is twenty-eight, and she is still a virgin."

There was an uncomfortable silence. Some of the interns snickered, but the senior officials of the company were quiet.

"That's right. I am," I piped up cheerfully. Some good soul mercifully changed the subject at that point.

Tatty and I ended up taking the same cab to the theater. "You know I really find it incredible that you live as a virgin. I would never give up the way I live even though it causes me so much pain. How do you do it? Frankly, I can't see why you do it, and I resent you for it," she said. I didn't reply since we had talked about the reasons for chastity before.

We got to the theater, and as usual, the play had sexual innuendos. The whole time Tatty and one of her friends kept looking over at me laughing and pointing.

It was quite uncomfortable at the time, but I can look back on it now and laugh. You have to know that many people may not have met someone like me before. They don't understand. They have never been taught correct principles.

66

The Battle Maidens of the Lord

⤟⤞

In spite of ridicule and attempted public humiliation, Olivia was able to keep her composure and equilibrium because of her understanding and faith in the principles of the Gospel of Christ. Olivia did not slink down in her seat, but bravely faced the situation, thereby making it of little consequence. A strong testimony of gospel principles, such as chastity and fidelity, is such a powerful aid in dealing with evil intent that the devil and his cohorts hardly have a chance to succeed.

Sometimes the devil is not involved in situations where lives can take a turn into trouble. Many situations in which women find themselves such as prolonged illness and poverty take courage to deal with on a daily basis. A constant steady pressure can be exerted upon individuals and families for years. The big push doesn't come followed by a rest period. Some people who are not going through this type of trial tend to forget about the people experiencing it because the problem never goes away. No one can rush in with a meal, say some kind words, and make it all better. There are those Christ-like persons who steadily earn a place in heaven by continual service. One such sister brought a meal once a week to a family who had a child born with a severe handicap until that child finally returned to his Heavenly Father years later. This lovely woman exhibited the pure love of Christ.

In the following story, another woman, Marin, learned to deal with the constant, unrelenting pressure of prolonged illness. These trials are not precipitated by

67

Jaqueline Ethington

Satan, but if it is permitted, he is happy to step in and make life worse.

GOING DOWN THE ROAD I DIDN'T WANT TO TAKE

When I was five and half months pregnant with our fifth child, I tripped and fell down steep stairs as I was going to do the laundry. I picked myself up, finished the laundry, and hobbled back up to my four little ones. Since I didn't break anything, I thought I must be all right. But I didn't feel well.

Five years after the accident, I was not able to get out of bed. Not only were my insides fractured and dislocated, but the baby I was pregnant with when I fell was having seizures. Most of the time she was like a little doll sitting still on the couch. At this point we found a doctor who tried to help us both. After one treatment, our daughter was able to play with her toys, open doors, and do things again. It was like putting life into a broken toy. But after several years, I realized I was not getting better.

One time I remember thinking that I wanted my mom to come and help me. I was feeling down and lonely. Most of the time, I would try to get along with just my family. I'll never forget that experience, that yearning for my mother to come.

She was doing genealogy work at the time, a lot of genealogy. Someone unseen came. I don't know who it was, but it was like they were speaking to me.

"Please. You're all right. You'll be OK. What your mother is doing is so important. Please don't ask her for her time," they said.

68

The Battle Maidens of the Lord

So I never made that phone call. You know what? We were all right. We were blessed. So many times I felt like our Heavenly Father was very aware of us. Perhaps some of those people that my mother was helping came and helped us out.

Every penny we had seemed to be spent going to see a doctor or buying a car. We wore out several cars driving to distant doctors every week for about fifteen years. Finally, a doctor in another state helped me get into what you would call a "normal range," where I am today. All in all, I spent twenty years feeling so badly that I couldn't play with my children, help them with their homework, or shop for prom dresses. Instead, my children spent their time taking care of me. Our family gained quite a polishing from that experience.

At one point my husband and I were thinking about going on a mission, and I would have to be without my doctor. So I went to the temple to discus it with the Lord.

"Well, you're going to have to show me how now," I said to the Lord.

I didn't get an answer so I went again. The temple was about four hours away from our home. From the minute I walked in the door until I left, I kept my mind praying to Him continually about the problem.

"Please, you've got to help me. I've got to move forward again," I pleaded.

When I got home that time, the information came to me so fast. Everything was coming to me about what

69

to do and how to do it. I was so grateful to receive that information. I was able to get better again from where I was.

Progress isn't straight up. It is in increments, like going up steps a little at a time. It is precept by precept, like the scriptures say, line upon line. That is how I was taught, and that is how I received information. When I truly sought for information from Him, it was given to me liberally. Whenever I would be content to stay where I was for a while, He would leave me there. It was really quite a learning process.

I had to deal with the fact that I had messed up my child's life when I fell. I had to go to my Heavenly Father to sort it out, to tell him how I was feeling, and that it was truly an accident. Our daughter still lives with us and will all of her life. It is a blessing for her that we live in a remote area. We've learned a lot about patience and a lot about listening. Isn't that what life is all about? Those traumatic experiences ended up being a blessing to our family.

During this illness I had many priesthood blessings which promised me that I would get well. However, I had a lot of fear, fear that I would never be better. I studied diligently about faith because I wanted to make sure that I had what it took to become well, that the Lord could heal me.

One time my husband was gone, and I was home alone. I was ill and not feeling strong physically. I had just put all the children to bed and had gone to bed myself when I felt the presence of an evil spirit. It felt to me like Satan was right there in my bedroom. I was grateful for the things that I had been taught as a young girl.

In the name of Jesus Christ I commanded him to leave. Of course, he left. I have always thought that the reason that the evil spirit came was because I was in a weakened condition. I had three experiences like that while I was getting well. Those were not happy experiences. I am grateful that I had the truth of the gospel in my life to help me.

Today I am a happy grandmother with twenty-two grandchildren. I can play with them and do a hard day's work. Sometimes when I see someone ill, I think about my experience.

"Well, you have to go down a road you didn't think you were going to want to take," I would say to myself.

Nobody wants to take time out for that road. You know what, when you go down it, and you get to the end, you are grateful for the things that you learned, especially if you have taken the Savior as your guide and friend.

Life's experiences take a brave heart to endure sometimes. Danielle needed a brave heart to cross a line she felt was required to demonstrate her opposition to coercion. Olivia needed a brave heart to deal with attempted public humiliation for her righteousness. Marin needed a brave heart to endure a prolonged illness without giving up hope and becoming despondent. All of us need a brave heart in this life to make it through troubles and temptations that will come our way. God has given us the weapons we need to bravely fight our way through. It is easier to remain brave if we remember the words of Christ. *In the world ye shall have tribulation: but be of good cheer; I have overcome the world.*[60]

Chapter 8

Weaponry

Wherefore, lift up your hearts and rejoice,
And gird up your loins, and take upon you my whole armor,
That ye may be able to withstand the evil day,
Having done all, that ye may be able to stand.
D&C 27:15[61]

The Lord has given many tools with which to fight against evil. God, being the ultimate in creativity, will help you in any situation the devil can devise. Arm yourself with the weapons God has given us. Here are a number of the weapons with which we fight, but this is by no means all of them.

PRAYER

Prayer is the weapon of first and last resort. There are so many situations in life about which we will need to be praying. Each person will have her own unique tests and challenges and therefore her own unique prayers. That is what is so good about prayer. It is so versatile. God is always listening and will come to the aid of His children in ways that only God can. Nothing that concerns us will seem unimportant to Him.

We will "receive answers through inspiration and revelation."[62] This was emphasized to Sandra when she

Jaqueline Ethington
was overwhelmed with all of her responsibilities. She
prayed to God for help, telling Him that she didn't see
how she could do it all. Soon after this prayer, she
received a telephone call. A mistake had been made, and
she didn't have to teach a lesson on Sunday. Sandra was
so relieved that she thanked God over and over. A calm
came over her, and all turned out well. Silly? Perhaps.
But it was important to her at the time. How much more
intently Heavenly Father must listen to our cries for help
in our truly desperate hours.

When we receive answers to our everyday prayers,
it gives us confidence that we will receive answers when
we ask under any circumstance. When prayers are
answered, we need to express our gratitude. We need to
be especially diligent in thanking Heavenly Father for His
loving care, for blessings, and for His wisdom in dealing
with our prayerful petitions.

ASKING FOR HELP
While serving in a position at church, Leslie
sometimes heard stories that broke her heart. They
weren't necessarily related to her particular church job.
One time she was praying mightily to know how to help a
certain family. It was a situation where hearts needed to
be changed and prison had to be endured. The
comforting influence of the Holy Ghost was desperately
required for that family.

One night she had a dream in which she was
shown the importance of praying for each other. In this
dream she was walking down a deep trench with hot coals

raining down on her from both sides. Leslie knew that
the extreme heat represented the extreme importance of
praying for each other. When she woke up, she felt like
she needed to jump across the room to get away from that
heat. She had a great desire to call the Relief Society
President of her ward and tell her that they all needed to
be praying for each other, that they should quit keeping
their problems to themselves, and should ask each other
for help through prayer.

Now Leslie lives in a different ward. Each Sunday
during opening exercises one of the members of the Relief
Society Presidency asks if there is anyone who needs the
prayers of her sisters in the coming week. As time has
gone by, more and more people ask for help through
prayers. They ask for help for their sick, for themselves,
for many different reasons. The prayers are working in
Leslie's ward. The sick are being healed. Strength and
help is coming from the Lord.

Prayer is one way to keep the baptismal covenant
to bear one another's burdens. There is a need for the
daughters of God to quit being so secretive about their
troubles and ask for the prayers of the saints. Of course,
there are some things that will need to be kept within
families, but in those cases, the family members need to
be praying for each other. *And, as it is written—Whatsoever
ye shall ask in faith, being united in prayer according to my
command, ye shall receive.*[63]

People love whom they pray for. Think about
that. It is safe to ask for the prayers of others in trials.

They will love the ones they pray for more and more, whatever the situation.

Janet found herself in a situation that she felt she couldn't handle, a situation in which many of us have found ourselves. She sought humbly through prayer for help.

HUMBLED

After a twenty-five year absence, I recently went back to college. I said to myself, "Janet, you can do this." But it was hard. An essay in my first English class was proving difficult for me. I didn't know how to go about it and felt inadequate. Company was coming, and there were many pressures in addition to the essay. However, I knew that Heavenly Father would help me.

Just to complete a paragraph, I would have to pray for help. It was such a hard essay for me. I struggled with it and with knowing how to do it.

After I turned in my paper, I spent a lot of time worrying about the grade that I was going to get and what my professor would have to say. Last night I went to class in trepidation to receive the results.

I gave myself a good pep talk. "OK. I'm going to get this paper that is all marked up. That's all right. I'll be learning."

I removed the cover sheet and looked at the first page. There were no marks on it. There were little comments like "great story' and "amusing." There was not a single mark on the whole essay. At the end, my professor wrote, "Outstanding essay. Don't change a thing." I was completely humbled. I had a perfect score.

The Battle Maidens of the Lord

❧

When Janet was faced with a problem that she didn't feel adequate to deal with, she went to her Father in Heaven for help. If we ask Him in prayer, God makes up for the lack in us, and makes us adequate for the task.

SCRIPTURES

Scripture study is another weapon we can use. Here is what the Lord says about his scriptures. *These words are not of men nor of man,...For it is my voice which speaketh them unto you; for they are given by my Spirit unto you, and by my power you can read them...; therefore, you can testify that you have heard my voice, and know my words.*[64]

Scripture study or the study of articles in the Latter-day Saint church magazines or church lesson books will bring the Holy Ghost and answers to prayers. They will also give us information that the Lord wants us to know. By reading the very words of God, comfort and peace will come. *...hear the pleasing word of God, yea, the word which healeth the wounded soul* (Jacob 2:8).[65] Sometimes thoughts which have never before entered your mind will come and bring solutions to problems. Many will discover things about themselves that they didn't know. Revelation will come to them. They will gather up to themselves strength and courage, knowledge and wisdom, hope and clear vision. *...Wherefore, I said unto you, feast upon the words of Christ; for behold, the words of Christ will tell you all things what ye should do.*[66]

Jaqueline Ethington

President Dallin H. Oaks tells us that through the scripture study we can obtain revelation. "The idea that scripture reading can lead to inspiration and revelation opens the door to the truth that a scripture is not limited to what it meant when it was written, but may also include what the scripture means to the reader today."[67]

PRIESTHOOD

The priesthood of God is a magnificent force upon the earth today, and it is a powerful agent in the fight against evil. "Priesthood is the authority and power which God has granted to men on earth to act for Him. When we exercise priesthood authority properly, we do what He would do if He were present."[68] Priesthood is a river of righteousness flowing over the earth. When this river reflects the flame of the Son's influence, brilliant flashes of light spark into being, giving enlightenment and hope to the world. This power resides in the hands of worthy men who lead and guide His church and bless His people. It also resides in the hands of the worthy boys and men who lead families and the local units of the church.

In these latter days when the priesthood is on the earth, the church functions under its influence. Members are baptized and given the gift of the Holy Ghost by the power of the priesthood. From then on, if they live worthily, the Holy Ghost will stay with them and guide them. The sacrament is blessed by the power of the priesthood, whereby if God's people will repent and always remember Christ, they will always have His spirit to be with

The Battle Maidens of the Lord

them. When members receive their endowments in the temple by the power of the priesthood, they are endowed with power from on high.[69] When couples are married in the temple for time and eternity by the power of the priesthood, they are sealed forever together as a family. If this couple lives worthily, they are given the promise of exaltation in the kingdom of our Heavenly Father. If one hears the missionaries and joins the Church of Jesus of Latter-day Saints, it is because the priesthood holders have sent missionaries out into the world.

Since the restoration of the priesthood, the world has become a very different place. The enlightening influence of the priesthood, the Holy Ghost, and the Light of Christ have moved many in the world to spiritual excellence. Likewise, since the restoration of the priesthood in 1830, the temporal world has moved from the horse and buggy age to the exploration of space. The return of the priesthood and the fullness of the gospel of Jesus Christ have exerted an influence on all of humanity whether they can recognize it or not. It is no accident that we have computers, telephones, airplanes, automobiles, abundant food supplies, huge medical advances, and material wealth. All these things and many more help in spreading the gospel throughout the earth as required by our Lord. The influence of the priesthood flows all around us, blessing our lives.

Do not neglect to ask for priesthood blessings, Sisters. These blessings will be a great enabling power, a protection and a comfort. They will bring healing and strength and many other blessings.

Jaqueline Ethington

THE LIGHT OF CHRIST

The Light of Christ is a defensive weapon that permeates the world. Satan is allowed to tempt us, but we are not without help. All people are born with the Light of Christ. The human conscience is one aspect of the Light of Christ. In the Garden of Eden, when Adam and Eve ate the forbidden fruit, they were given to know good from evil. That is a trait inherent in all of their descendents. How could anyone use their agency if they did not know the difference between good and evil? *Search diligently in the light of Christ that ye may know good from evil; and if ye will lay hold upon every good thing, and condemn it not, ye certainly will be a child of Christ.*[70]

"If we understand the reality of the Light of Christ... within ourselves, and understand the great challenge that we have—the surroundings in which we live, the danger which sometimes besets us—we will have courage and inspiration beyond that which we have known heretofore."[71]

All people need to tap into the power of the Light of Christ. It is like a sunbeam from heaven shining directly upon us all of the time. We are encased in its light and power. It follows us everywhere we go and never leaves us. We cannot see it, just as we cannot see ultraviolet light with our natural eyes. Nevertheless, it is there. When we realize this, we can go forward in courage because we are never alone. If we keep God's commandments and live as well as we can, then we can expect and receive inspiration and revelation because we have a direct line to heaven. These heavenly helps can be beamed to us instantaneously, so to speak. For reasons known to God, this may not always be the case, but it can and does happen often. If information or comfort or what is needed is not sent instantly when asked, it is sent instantly when God finds it expedient to do so.

...*Through Jesus Christ his Son—he that ascended up on high, as also he descended below all things, in that he comprehended all things, that he might be in all and through all things, the light of truth; which truth shineth. This is the light of Christ....And the light which shineth, which giveth you light, as through him who enlighteneth your eyes which is the same light that quickeneth your understandings; which light proceedeth from the presence of God to fill the immensity of space.*[72]

THE HOLY GHOST

The Holy Ghost is another partner for those who battle for good. Anyone on earth who seeks to know Heavenly Father and His Son, Jesus Christ, will receive the Holy Ghost. And if they are willing to open their hearts to the influence of that Holy Spirit, they will receive knowledge of the divinity of the Godhead, Heavenly Father, Jesus Christ and the Holy Ghost.

All can receive the Holy Ghost from time to time, but the gift of the Holy Ghost comes only to those who have been baptized and receive this gift through the laying on of hands by men holding the priesthood and proper authority from God. If baptismal covenants are kept, by repenting and keeping the commandments of God, by taking on His name, and by bearing one another's burdens, the baptized will always have the Spirit of Christ

Jaqueline Ethington

and the Holy Ghost to be with them. As they grow in righteousness and understanding, this dear and Holy Spirit, the third member of the Godhead, will be felt more and more keenly.

The following scriptures show only a small part of the breadth of help and the gifts that we can receive through the Holy Ghost. God's children will be *filled...with the spirit of God, in wisdom, and in understanding.*[73] They will be able to confess *by the...Holy Ghost that Jesus is the Christ.*[74] They will walk *in the comfort of the Holy Ghost.*[75] The *Holy Ghost...shall teach you all things and bring all things to your remembrance.*[76] They teach *not in the words which man's wisdom teacheth, but which the Holy Ghost teacheth.*[77] *Men (and women) of God spake (speak) as they were (are) moved by the Holy Ghost.*[78] The *Holy Ghost will show you all things ye should do.*[79] These gifts from the Holy Ghost enable mankind and womankind to be more than they naturally are.

The children of God are here on earth to fulfill their missions and help their families and all of humanity win the battle Satan is raising against them. One of the best defenses against Satan is the gift of the Holy Ghost. God, (that is to say Heavenly Father, Jesus Christ, and the Holy Ghost working together in complete unity of purpose), is their Battle Mate.

These words by the Prophet Brigham Young concerning the Holy Ghost epitomize the beauty of that gift. "So live every morning, noon, and evening, every moment, as to enjoy the Holy Ghost continually. Do not deprive yourselves of this privilege, brethren and sisters;

The Battle Maidens of the Lord
then you can see, hear, and understand, and know things that are of God, the visible and invisible, in heaven and on earth~things past, present, and to come. No power can deprive you of this privilege, and God will bless you, and we will bask in his presence with our Elder Brother, and with all the sons and daughters of Adam who have been redeemed from the four quarters of the earth, to live for ever."[80]

OBEDIENCE

Another weapon against Satan is obedience to God's commandments. If commandments are obeyed, Satan will not be allowed to overpower the Lord's servants. *And I said unto them...whoso would hearken unto the word of God, and would hold fast unto it, they would never perish; neither would the temptations and fiery darts of the adversary over power them unto blindness, to lead them away to destruction.*[81]

It is important that we learn what the commandments are. A diligent study of the scriptures will lead us to a thorough knowledge of the subject. If we are just starting out on the journey to learn the gospel and the commandments, then the Ten Commandments are a good place to start. If our actions are based on love and respect for our God, our families, and our fellow folk, we will be doing well.

Even with all we can do to avoid breaking the commandments and to avoid sin, there are still situations that cause us grief because of our human condition. For example, while working with a group of righteous women

83

doing a service project, Julie made an innocent comment, which caused someone distress. She felt very badly. You don't need temptations to make mistakes. Mistakes are just mistakes, and they can cause plenty of suffering. Sins are an entirely different matter. Repenting is a painful process. It is easier to do what is right to begin with. Learn what the commandments are and obey them. The rewards are great because the obedient will receive all that the Father has and will have the guiding spirit of the Holy Ghost. Jesus said, *He that hath my commandments, and keepeth them, he it is that loveth me: and he that loveth me shall be loved of my Father, and I will love him, and will manifest myself to him* (or her).[82]

MUSIC

Good music can be used to fight evil. Uplifting music invites the Holy Spirit. When listening to the lovely tones of inspired music, it seems like it is easier for the Spirit to reach the listeners, to teach them. Revelation is a mighty weapon against the adversary. Revelation will come when we use any of the weapons discussed in this book to gain victory over the enemy. Listening to good music and contemplating our situation just happens to be a particularly pleasant way to receive communication from the Holy Ghost. A righteous person listening to beautiful or spiritual music will often find a wonderful conduit to the powers of heaven.

Hymns bring comfort and the feeling of God's love. Those listening or singing receive messages to guide them and heal their hearts. When worshipers truly

The Battle Maidens of the Lord concentrate on the words of hymns, the Holy Ghost tends to rush in and fill their beings with love and light.

Emilie, a lovely young lady with a beautiful voice, tried hard to develop her musical talents. At one point she heard a voice say, "Sing for me." She sang often in church and many people commented on the sweet, comforting spirit that could be felt through her songs.

SING FOR ME

Music, the wind that pushes the soul along
Like a ship over the sea,
Ruffles the veil of eternity.
Sing for me.

MIND CONTROL

Mind control is another weapon that can be used against Satan. He certainly uses it against us. One of the weapons that Satan uses against the children of God is negative and destructive thought. He whispers mean things into the mind and through such messages nudges people in the wrong direction. As church leaders have counseled, it is a good idea to choose a hymn to sing in the mind or out loud when accosted by garbage thoughts. A righteous diversion is needed. It is important to use agency and divert the mind back onto a productive course of thinking. In the following story, Zena became gifted in the art of diversion.

DECIEVED

When I was young, I was greatly offended. I

Jaqueline Ethington

would often think with anger about the offence and the person who offended me, but most especially when I was ironing. Finally, I chose not to let this offence ruin my life and tried to forgive the offender. I prayed frequently about it. This anger was deeply entrenched from years of permissiveness on my part. I had permitted myself to be deceived by Satan by dwelling on this negative experience.

After I realized what was happening, I took any step necessary to put an end to it. Whenever angry thoughts came into my mind, I did whatever it took to immediately cast them out. When I ironed, I would watch a favorite movie. I needed something totally mind absorbing that lasted for the duration of the task. If I wasn't ironing when angry thoughts came, I would quickly pick up a good book and start reading. Eventually I got to the point where I could sing a hymn and forget my anger. Then I was able to forgive. It has been a blessing to be free of that heavy burden.

Eventually Zena recognized what was happening to her. Many women think that such thoughts are just a natural outcome of a flawed character. This is not the case because these thoughts can be controlled. Dwelling on angry thoughts or a perceived offence is the work of the devil. He will whisper reminders to a woman of offences or angers and the like if he can, and if she doesn't control her thoughts, Satan will lead her into a swamp of destructive thinking.

The evil one also has a habit of whispering terrible things about his victim into her mind. He says things like this: you are fat, you're ugly, nobody likes you, you are so stupid, why did you say that, idiot. He adds in things like these: you have no talent, who do you think you are, nobody cares what you think, God won't talk to you, you are worthless. The list goes on and on. This is the devil's way of disabling Heavenly Father's children. This is his way of making sure the daughters of God don't complete their missions and that they fall into his dirty hands.

If negative thoughts are running through the mind, it is certain that they come from Satan. God loves his children, and He wouldn't do that to them. Satan does not love them, and he bombards people all the time with negative messages. God's children are stronger than the evil villain. They have the power to throw the rascal out. Part of the reason that Satan has been able to do this is because women have been permissive in their thinking. They have permitted Satan to do this. Now is the time to forbid it. The following is one process by which the daughters of God can take back control of their thoughts.

Whenever destructive thoughts come into your mind, here is what you can do.

1. Say, "I am a daughter of God, and He loves me." Put a big emphasis on the words "I" and "He."

2. Think of a spiritual experience when you received instruction or comfort, when you knew God was aware of you and loved you. We all have such experiences. By searching your heart and mind, you can find them. It could be a dream, a whispering of peace or comfort, inspiration, or protection. It could be so many

87

different things.

     3. In your mind, you can go to a sacred place such as a temple or another location dear to you and rest your heart and mind there in the peace of Christ until you have recovered your true daughter of God self.

     4. Sing a hymn.

     5. Watch a good movie or call a friend.

     6. Quickly pick up the scriptures or a church magazine or another type of good book and start reading.

     7. Pray. Don't be proud. Ask for help in overcoming Satan's influence. Whenever there is even a hint of his influence, immediately start praying for guidance, strength, and protection.

     8. Ask your Heavenly Father to let you know that he loves you, that you are important to Him, and then listen to His answer.

     9. Act immediately. You can run interference by occupying your mind with something else uplifting, anything else that isn't detrimental to you. Don't indulge in permissive thinking by listening to the evil things Satan is putting into your mind. You've developed bad habits. Don't indulge in them. Satan will laugh with glee if you do.

     The daughters of God have to deal with permissive thinking decisively. It is important that we reinforce our eternal heritage. God is our Father, and He loves us. He created the universe and everything in it. He loved us enough to create spirit bodies for us and then send us to earth to receive mortal bodies. He made the Plan of Salvation so that we could come home to Him,

The Battle Maidens of the Lord

wrapped in immortality and eternal life. He has spent a lot of love, time, and talent on us, and we are precious to Him. It will break His heart if He loses any of His dear daughters or sons.

We shouldn't let Satan sabotage us with destructive thoughts thereby stopping or slowing the progress that will lead us back to Him. *Therefore, cheer up your hearts, and remember that ye are free to act for yourselves— to choose the way of everlasting death or the way of eternal life*.[83]

Some may think this is a strange way to overcome negative thoughts, but it is not. Once the daughters of God realize that God, that great and Eternal Being, truly loves us, not in theory but in reality~that we are His children~we will be able to truly love ourselves. All that negativism just slides away. We will have strength within ourselves. When the devil tries his old tricks, we will ignore them. Then one day, we will realize that we are now ignoring his jabs and taunts, and it will surprise us. We will have changed without being aware of it. Now the heavenly daughters will move forward in the strength and power of the Lord.

In the scriptures, God has laid out for His children exactly what would be a good thought process to follow. He tells His family that whatsoever things are true, honest, just, pure, lovely or of good report; if there be any virtue or any praise, think on these things.[84] Have faith. All good things are possible.

FAITH

Faith in Christ is a critical weapon against evil.

Faith in Christ is the principle upon which all of God's children operate. It is a principle that moves people to action. *Faith is not to have a perfect knowledge of things; therefore if ye have faith ye hope for things which are not seen, which are true.*[85]

Because of faith, Queen Esther of <u>Old Testament</u> fame had the courage to go before the king to save her people. She could have suffered execution for such an act. During the time of Christ, a woman of faith touched the hem of Jesus' garment and was healed of an issue of blood. When men and women in foreign lands, such and England and Sweden, joined the church in the nineteenth century, they had a great desire to gather with the saints in America. Their faith in Christ gave them the will and ability to do so. A multitude of righteous souls came across the ocean and strengthened the church greatly upon their arrival.

Faith enables the young mothers of today to hunt up all the Sunday shoes on a Sunday morning and deal with the confusion and whining as she hustles the children out the door to Church. Then during Sacrament meeting, she does her best to exercise her faith and patience when her children talk out loud, when her four year old rolls under the pew, and when the occasional crying breaks out for reasons best left to speculation. And through it all, she never turns around to see who is watching her circus extravaganza. It takes great faith to continue doing a difficult task with few immediate rewards. As it happens, those same active children whose parents took them to church every Sunday

The Battle Maidens of the Lord

in turn gain testimonies of the restored Gospel of Christ and take their own bouncy bunch of boys and girls to church regularly. There are many ways that women can use the power of faith to bless their families and others. Faith enables women to do great and noble things.

Joseph Smith said, "No matter who believeth, these signs, such as healing the sick, casting out devils, etc., should follow all that believe, whether male or female."[86] Women do not have the priesthood or the responsibility for the administration of the church, but they do have great spiritual power through faith in Christ. This knowledge, that faith brings power, is an enabling strength to the Battle Maidens of these days. The knowledge that faith in Christ is the power that women can use for their benefit, and for the benefit, of others gives courage and hope.

At this time the priesthood and its power surrounds the women of the church in abundance. They can call upon the priesthood for blessings and help on every side. The time may come when women may not be so fortunate and will have to use the power of their faith even more strongly than they do now. There may be any number of special circumstances where women could be on their own. They might be single and living far from any branch of the church. Husbands may be away from home when there is an emergency. War, one of the plagues of the last days, may cause a separation from priesthood holders. Few women have given a blessing of healing, nor would they if the priesthood were available. But it is important to know that if it is necessary, women

91

can bless through the power of faith. "Respecting females administering for the healing of the sick, he (Joseph Smith, Jr.) further remarked, there could be no evil in it, if God gave His sanction by healing; that there could be no more sin in any female laying hands on and praying for the sick, than in wetting the face with water, it is no sin for anybody to administer that has faith, or if the sick have faith to be healed by their administration."[86]

Through faith women can cast out devils. It is nice to know and good to do. A young father taught his eight-year-old daughter what to do if any evil spirit should bother her. "You need to pray in the name of Jesus Christ for the evil spirit to leave," he said to her. Joseph Smith taught that, "They who have tabernacles (bodies), have power over those who have not."[87] Teach your sons and daughters these principles. They need to know them. Children will not often be bothered. But the knowledge needs to be planted in their minds early, so it can be called upon whenever the need may arise later. Children need to be empowered by your teachings to cast out devils so that they will not be overcome with fear and confusion if they are ever approached by the evil and greedy beings. Moses had to command the devil to leave four times before he finally did.[88] Sometimes a person may also need to be persistent, but because of the authority of Christ, the devil must leave. Put this information into your spiritual war-bag. Have it ready and waiting there for the time of battle.

Through faith women can do all things that are expedient in the Lord. ...*The Lord is able to do all things according to his will for the children of men, if it so be that they exercise faith in him.*[89]   Madeline tells the story of her Mother, who knew how to use the power of faith in her life.

STORM CLOUDS

The many experiences that I've had with faith all tie back to my mother. She was raised in a little Mormon colony up in the mountains of Mexico. They didn't have stores, and they didn't have doctors. The saints had to completely rely on the priesthood and on the Spirit. Everyday their life was one of faith. They relied on the Lord to help them in everything. So it became something that they were used to. It wasn't strange to them.

Growing up in Mexico, if my brothers and sisters and I lost something, or if we were having trouble with a friend, or whatever the situation might be, we would go to Mom.

"Well, did you pray and ask Heavenly Father?" she would ask.

My mother taught me about faith and about prayer, and with that came the knowledge that my prayers would be answered.

One experience that really stands out to me about my mother happened when we were preparing for a wedding reception. My brother had met a beautiful young woman from the United States of America. Her family was wealthy. My parents were not and struggled financially. They wanted to have a nice reception for my brother and his lovely bride, so we worked hard on the yard and decorated a tennis court.

We lived in a flat valley with a lot of farms. You could see quite a way to the horizon and mountains. Dark storm clouds would move in with sheets of water pounding down across the earth. Often we watched their progress across the landscape. On this particular afternoon, one of those storms came rolling in. The wedding reception was doomed. My mother disappeared into the house and prayed. When she came out, we watched a miracle happen. That storm literally took a sharp turn and went off in a different direction. Her faith had turned the storm.

SPIRITUAL GIFTS

Spiritual gifts are another weapon that can be used so effectively in the battle against evil. Elder Bruce R. McConkie told us at the dedication of the Monument to Women in Nauvoo that as far as spiritual gifts were concerned "men and women stand in a position of absolute equality before the Lord. He is no respecter of persons nor of sexes, and he blesses those men and those women who seek him and serve him and keep his commandments."[90]

And it shall come to pass... that I will pour out of my spirit upon all flesh; and your sons and your daughters shall prophesy, your old men shall dream dreams, your young men shall see visions.[91]

God has mentioned more then once in the scriptures that his daughters can be blessed with spiritual manifestations. So that there will be no misunderstanding

The Battle Maidens of the Lord

of this fact, He says the following. *And on my servants and on my handmaidens I will pour out in those days of my Spirit; and they shall prophesy.*[92] This is not to say that women can be the prophet of the church. That is a priesthood calling. Women, however, can have the gift of prophesy. For example, *The testimony of Jesus is the spirit of prophesy.*[93] That passage is plain enough for all to understand. Spiritual gifts that women have are to be used for the benefit of their families and for use in their stewardships here upon the earth. The gift of prophesy does not only mean knowing things of the future, although that may happen, it also means that they will receive spiritual knowledge, godly knowledge. Sometimes knowledge will be given at the very moment a woman opens her mouth to speak, if it is needed. It means sometimes receiving knowledge of things as they were, as they are, and as they will be.[94] *And now, he imparteth his word by angels unto men, yea, not only men but women also. Now this is not all; little children do have words given unto them many times, which confound the wise and the learned.*[95]

Other spiritual gifts that can be received are faith, faith to heal, and faith to be healed. A testimony of the truthfulness of the gospel of Christ and of the divinity of Christ is a gift that must be shared with others. Teaching the word of knowledge is another gift. The word of wisdom is a gift, or in other words, understanding through experience and the voice of the Spirit. Revelation is a spiritual gift that women can all have and desperately need in these times. "The power of discernment is essential if we are to distinguish between

95

genuine spiritual gifts and the counterfeits Satan seeks to use to deceive men and women and thwart the work of God."[96] Also, the Lord can give the gift of discerning the character of certain people. Live righteously and seek for those spiritual gifts that will help in the battles of life. There are many different spiritual gifts, and some of those gifts are quite unusual. The great number of possible gifts is simply unknowable except to God.

Only a few of the weapons that we can use against evil are mentioned here. It is important to became familiar with each of these weapons and understand how to use them. These weapons need to be ingrained into your being through practice and constant use. That way, when they are needed, they will be second nature to the Battle Maidens, and the Battle Maidens will not be overwhelmed in a surprise attack by the evil one. Each weapon will be needed at some time. Prayer and scripture study are two things that will bring knowledge of and obedience to the commandments as well as bring the companionship of the Holy Ghost. Good works through faith will bring increased acquisition of spiritual gifts. Understanding of a woman's relationship to the priesthood and the blessings of the priesthood are important to bring about the maximum benefit from this great power. And then there is the fact that women are always encased in the Light of Christ for added confidence. Directing your thoughts in a righteous course is a powerful principle in the fight against Satan's attempts to destroy God's daughters. Good music, that sweet element that enables the Holy Ghost to come to

The Battle Maidens of the Lord
you in a heavenly environment, can bring spiritual companionship and help. These gifts and many more have been given in love to Father's children to enable them to successfully return to Him.

Stand therefore, having your loins girt about with truth, having on the breastplate of righteousness, and your feet shod with the preparation of the gospel of peace, which I have sent mine angels to commit unto you; taking the shield of faith wherewith ye shall be able to quench all the fiery darts of the wicked; and take the helmet of salvation, and the sword of my Spirit, which I will pour out upon you, and my word which I reveal unto you, and be agreed as touching all things whatsoever ye ask of me, and be faithful until I come, and ye shall be caught up that where I am ye shall be also. Amen.[97]

Chapter 9

Attack

And Christ said: If ye will have faith in me
Ye shall have power to do
Whatsoever thing is expedient in me
Moroni 7:33[98]

Sometimes Satan will launch an all out direct attack against the valiant Battle Maidens of the Lord, hoping to overpower them. They need not be unduly afraid.

And whoso shall ask it in my name in faith, they shall cast out devils.[99] As we have already discussed, this applies to women and children as well as men. These faithful women whose stories are in this chapter have had occasion to do this. By using the name of Jesus Christ, they have been given the power to cast out Satan and his cohorts. The following is a poem that tells of the experience of one woman who learned the power of the name of deity.

BECAUSE I LOVE

I had a dream wherein an evil spirit came.
Why do you do these things, he said.
Why do you keep the commandments of God, he meant.

The Battle Maidens of the Lord
"Because I love,' I said.
"I love my husband and my children.
I love my Heavenly Father and Jesus Christ."
At the name of God, he fled
Like a streak of lightening falling from heaven.

Battle Maidens need to be prepared no matter where they find themselves. Dianne experienced the fight of her life twenty thousand feet over the Atlantic Ocean.

I WANTED TO KNOW

I was on an airplane coming back from Denmark with my daughter and wanted to read through the <u>Book of Mormon</u>. I love plane rides because nobody can bother you. You can just sit and read.

"This is perfect," I thought.

I almost got through the book that time. I remember reflecting upon my life. We've all sinned, and I just wanted to know if I had been forgiven. I had a strong desire to know that. I had read so many beautiful stories about Enos and Alma the Younger being forgiven of their sins, and I was impressed to ask. I knew that I had been forgiven, but I wanted to know again. You know how we are. We all fall short. Satan loves to deceive us and make us think that maybe we aren't ever going to get back to God.

After praying for a long time, I heard the sweetest voice in my mind that said, "Why do you doubt? Your sins are forgiven. Why do you doubt?" I just sat there with tears running down my face.

Then I had an experience where the adversary came and tried to overpower me. He started in on me immediately after I had had the sweetest experience of my life. It wasn't but a few minutes later that I had the doubts and the darkness.

"Did He say that? Is it true? Did I hear it," I thought. It was horrible. It was dark. It was a place I didn't ever want to be. "How can this be? How can I feel so good and then, all of a sudden, feel so powerless?"

There I was on a plane with people around and having this emotional experience. I got my composure and remember thinking, "Oh no you don't. I know heard it. It was real. I know it. You get away. Get thee hence, Satan." I had to make a conscious effort and pray in the name of Jesus Christ for Satan to leave. And he did.

We are human and are subject to all of mortality. We can't let Satan win. We can't, and he won't. We know the end. Read Revelation. The scroll is all done. It is finished. Satan does not win, and we know that. We need to be on the Lord's side. If we are not, we are going to lose, too.

Dianne's experience demonstrates something that can happen after we have a significant spiritual experience. Satan will try to come in and exert his influence to counterbalance God. The devil did the same to Christ after He returned from forty days of communing with His Father in Heaven. It is an old trick. However, we need not be deceived. We have the tools at hand to defeat him. The weapons discussed in the

The Battle Maidens of the Lord
previous chapter are always with us. The following is the
story of Felicia and her great faith, a faith that saved her.

I COULD FEEL HIS LOVE

Today we live in the United States of America, but
a few years ago my sister and I vacationed at a secluded
condo on a beach in Mexico. We were born in the
interior of Mexico and enjoyed visiting some of the
beautiful places around the country. Every morning we
would go running on the beach. One particular morning
my sister got busy in the house, so I went on ahead. As I
was running, I wasn't paying much attention to what was
going on around me. I was looking for shells and found
two big beautiful specimens.

When I got clear around the bay, I found a whole
pack of angry dogs. It was unusual for dogs to be angry
like that. I realized that I was in a precarious situation.
Trying to control my fear, I turned around and started
walking away.

There were a couple of sleek, sophisticated dogs, a
German shepherd, and a bunch of mongrels. One of the
sleek dogs came up and bit me. I turned around and
tried to scare them away by throwing my shells. This
infuriated them more. They organized into a circle
around me. There was a sleek lead dog barking right in
my face. The German shepherd and his companions
were circling in the middle. The outside ring was
composed of barking mongrels. The middle dogs were
quieter and would come in and bite.

Jaqueline Ethington

At this point I realized that they were indeed going to kill me. I almost felt like I was a child again. I could remember my mother teaching me to pray. I could remember the faith I felt as a child and what a power it was. I said a simple prayer asking for help. The dogs seemed to me almost like they were possessed, like evil spirits. It was a very frightening experience. It seemed like I was confronted with the powers of hell and not just angry dogs.

They knocked me down, and an unseen being lifted me up. Then I thought that I'd go out into the water and escape into the sea. However, there was a big sandbar where I was. The dogs followed me into the water and knocked me down again. Once again I was lifted up by unseen hands. I was overcome with a feeling of profound love~such as I had never felt before~and I knew that my Father in Heaven was protecting me. He was protecting me, and I could feel His love for me.

It wasn't quite my time to die yet. A rowboat came up to me, and two fishermen pulled me into the boat and beat off the dogs with their paddles. They had a jug of water in the boat and washed my wounds. It was a miracle that I didn't receive any bites above my waist. As they rowed back toward my condo, we stopped my sister from also running into the dog pack.

In that little town they had a medical clinic. In Mexico, when doctors are finished with their studies, they are sent out to do service for a year. Two young doctors were in that clinic doing their service. They dressed my wounds and took very good care of me. I complained to them about the scars that I would have.

"If you were a man," said one of the doctors, "those would be your trophies."

When we went to the little clinic, the people there and in the fishing village and the condos wanted us to go to the state police and tell them what had happened. They were concerned about the dog situation. Many children, and some adults, had been bitten by those wild dogs.

I went into the reception area of the police office with a shirt on and a towel wrapped around my waist. They had given me painkillers so I was feeling fine. But the doctors didn't stitch up those wounds because they wanted them to be cleaned out by draining. In a few minutes there were pools of blood on the floor. The secretaries panicked. They called Hermosillo and every agency they could think of. Before long, the dog attack was a huge event.

That night in the town you could hear cars going down the streets with loud speakers warning everyone to tie up their pet dogs because the army was coming the next day. In the morning, the army came with a machine gun and killed eighty rogue dogs.

There in that clinic they didn't have the resources to do rabies shots. My sister and I took one of the nurses with us, and we went to the city of Hermosillo to get the shots. Saliva had been dripping from the mouths of my attackers.

In Mexico, you don't have to make appointments with doctors. You wait in a line. There are many poor people who wait all day long in a line to get medical care. Since I was a tourist, and the attack was a notorious event, they took us right in. The nurse was able to get the materials she needed to bless that little town with vaccine for a lot of children. She also got rabies vaccine for those who had been bitten. That made me feel good, and it turned out well in the end.

When I returned to my home in the USA, my cousin came over to visit me. She made a comment that rang true to me.

"Maybe Satan was having a hard time getting at you in other ways so you were attacked by the dogs," she said.

Satan can attack you in many different ways. He can send evil spirits, vicious dogs, violent or seductive entertainment and people, or deceived family members. There are many ways to attack. If we keep the commandments of God, we will not be overcome. Even to start on the path of righteousness is to have the protection and inspiration of the Lord. In the next story, Cassandra was assaulted in her home. But as young as she was in the gospel, she and her husband still prevailed.

BLESS THIS HOUSE

I was baptized at eight years of age, but my parents didn't raise me in the Church. When I reached my teenage years, I made some bad choices and had a child out of wedlock.

104

The Battle Maidens of the Lord

Eventually, I met my husband. When we began to get serious, he told me that he would only marry in the temple.

"What's a temple?" I asked.

While we were engaged, we went to the temple preparation classes. I learned more about the church—things more wonderful than I could ever have imagined, and I began to gain a testimony of its truthfulness.

Several months later we were married in the temple for time and all eternity. In the days following our marriage, every night while going to sleep I could feel someone watching me. After about two months of not being able to sleep—feeling this uncomfortable evil feeling—I told my husband that I couldn't take it anymore. He was going to have to trade places with me.

We decided that we needed to say a prayer and bless the house. As we prayed, I could actually feel a physical being leaving. I knew when it was gone and did not have any more problems.

I believe Satan had had me for a long time and realized that I had moved toward the Lord with my life. He was trying to get me back. How thankful I am to have the protection of God. The inspiration He gives me helps me have courage to do anything He asks of me. I have reflected on this experience many times throughout my life. It makes me realize that Satan is present if we let him be. The Lord is even closer if we but listen to Him and keep His commandments. When we welcome Christ in, Satan has no hold on us.

———◆———

With malice and determination, Satan will attack the human family. One need not be unduly afraid. Have courage. God is infinitely more powerful than any evil spirit. The children of God need only to have faith and call upon their Heavenly Father in the name of Jesus Christ for help and protection.

Chapter 10

Ambushing the Enemy

Have not I commanded thee?
Be strong and of good courage;
Be not afraid, neither be thou dismayed:
For the Lord thy God is with thee whithersoever thou goest.
Joshua 1:9[100]

The Lord insulates and protects some of his most valiant sons and daughters in anonymity. They quietly go about doing the work of the kingdom—great and noble things—not arousing too much attention because of the seemingly ordinary nature of their actions. Perhaps the enemies of righteousness sometimes become a little complacent around them. It isn't that these quiet saints don't have trials and temptations; they do, but they are protected somewhat by their circumstances.

Sometimes it seems that Satan believes that the beautiful, socially adept, and obviously talented must be the Lord's greatest emissaries, and he turns the big guns on them. To their eternal glory these righteous people, who may indeed be great ambassadors of the Lord, manage mostly to come through the rain of fire valiantly. But there are secret weapons hidden away. These secret weapons are the hidden people who do not attract much attention in their early years. God works quietly in their hearts and minds preparing them for a great work.

This inner spiritual working on the soul for God's purposes is the case for many women that are alive today. Sherri Dew, a former member of the Relief Society General Presidency, was shy as a child. But when the time was right, the Lord helped Sherri overcome this and reach her godly potential. The Lord protects some young women from the inappropriate attention of the world by giving them a good dose of shyness or awkwardness in social situations. To teenagers, this may seem like a curse, but in the end it turns out to be a blessing because it often protects them from getting into situations where virtue might be compromised or standards lowered. There are many methods that the Lord uses to protect His children in their formative years. One young woman anguished over her crippled body and cried to the Lord asking Him why this had to be. She received the revelation that she had chosen this in the pre-mortal world rather than be subject to temptations she didn't think she could resist.

At the right time, God brings forth his hidden treasures, and with them He concentrates withering fire against the enemies of all that is good and holy. These women may surprise everyone but God and their parents by becoming magnificently righteous and stunningly effective in their callings to do good and serve the human family.

The same children of God who seemed quiet and shy are able to bring many souls to Christ. They are

The Battle Maidens of the Lord

humble and capable missionaries. They are loving parents and caring neighbors. They are primary teachers and girl's camp specialists. They can be talk show hosts, politicians, writers, artists, florists, candy makers, homemakers or anyone who has the will to fight for the right. When they, with their special talents and abilities, are revealed and their great work is commenced, Satan's guns will be turned against those who have ambushed his forces. However, they are righteous and strong, and Satan will have a hard time with them.

Joseph Smith, Jr., was just such a hidden treasured person. When you think of him, how can you ever look at any disheveled boy with a bad haircut and pants too short for his legs as anything but the godly, secret weapon that he is? To be sure, awkward or prissy young girls are also hidden treasures just waiting to come forth.

It is likely that Satan doesn't know where God has hidden his great and noble spirits until they do something that reveals their whereabouts. This is powerful protection for His servants until they are strong enough and ready to fulfill their missions upon the earth. In their youth, they learn by prayer, study, and experience. This is the pattern that He follows when he is preparing a person for an important purpose. For example, Christ's childhood and young adulthood has been shielded from prying eyes, and probably, to most people who knew Him then, His younger life seemed like nothing spectacular. The Holy Bible only states that He grew and became strong in spirit and wisdom.

Jaqueline Ethington

Joseph Smith's youth was similar to Christ's in some ways. Since more is known about his childhood, it can be seen that he led the ordinary life of a frontier child of his day. He was one of the hidden people. But God was preparing him to do a great work. The Lord was working on the inside of Joseph where others could not see. When Joseph Smith, Jr. went into the grove to pray, only then did Satan realize where the great prophet was, and only then did Satan come against Joseph with all his power. Before this time, Joseph probably looked like any other poor, gangly, farm boy destined to sow seeds in his fields and harvest crops of wheat and corn rather than sow the seeds of the restored Gospel of Christ and reap a great harvest of souls for God.

Satan's saboteurs are the mean-minded, conformist individuals who follow him. They can be sinister, sarcastic, cunning, dangerous, and petty. Paul described these people for us. *This know also, that in the last days perilous times shall come. For men (and women) shall be lovers of their own selves, covetous, boasters, proud, blasphemers, disobedient to parents, unthankful, unholy, without natural affection, trucebreakers, false accusers, incontinent, fierce, despisers of those that are good, traitors, heady, highminded, lovers of pleasures more than lovers of God; having a form of godliness; but denying the power thereof: from such turn away. For of this sort are they which creep into houses* (some television programs, some internet chat rooms, some romance novels, some people) *and lead captive silly women leaden with sins, led away with divers lusts, ever learning, and never able to come to the knowledge of the truth.*[101] This

110

The Battle Maidens of the Lord
scripture describes our times and the characteristics of the
followers of Satan. Their plan is to subvert society in
general but especially womankind, the protectors of
family values and the traditions of the mothers.

Satan and his followers have been ambushed
when their plans are thwarted. When their plans to
legalize unholy marriages are stopped, they have been
ambushed. When a law designed to stop abortions is
passed, they have been ambushed. When women don't
take the ever present bate to become morally
compromised, evil has been ambushed. When families
retrieve their wayward children, the devil has been
ambushed. When people repent, the devil has been
ambushed. When the children of God listen to the
missionaries and are baptized, Lucifer has been
ambushed. When families have family prayer, scripture
study, and family home evening, Satan has been
ambushed. Whenever Satan does not get his way, he has
been ambushed by diligent, righteous souls.

Things will become more and more difficult as
Lucifer, in desperation, mounts his final attack. But
Christ will sustain and angels will assist the good women
of the church and the world who ambush Satan and his
followers. Lucifer desires the physical and spiritual
destruction of all humankind. The Battle Maidens whom
God has hidden will be brought out of obscurity to join
in this great battle against evil.

The prophet Enoch was one of the hidden people.
He was a righteous follower of the family tradition of
preaching and prophesying to the people, probably

Jaqueline Ethington

without much success. For when the Lord came to Enoch asking him to prophesy unto the people and call them to repentance, Enoch bowed himself before the Lord and said, *Why is it that I have found favor in thy sight, and am but a lad, and all people hate me: for I am slow of speech; wherefore am I thy servant.*[102] The Lord told him to do the work he was commanded to do and then comforted him by telling him that no man would pierce him. The power to move mountains and turn the course of rivers was given to Enoch. He cried repentance unto the people, and all men were offended by him. However, *all nations feared greatly, so powerful was the word of Enoch, and so great was the power of the language which God had given him.*[103] The Lord gives his servants the talents and abilities to do His work as he has commanded them to do. The Lord brings His protected ones out of obscurity, and they perform their part in His marvelous plan.

Enoch continued his preaching among the wicked. In time the people whom he gathered around him became so righteous that God himself came down and dwelt with them in their city, Zion. After three hundred and sixty-five years, Zion and her inhabitants were lifted up to dwell with God. This was a definitive ambush of the evil one.

There are people who do a great work in the Kingdom of God, and they are easy to see because of their prominence. But there are also the hidden people, those who are behind the scenes, sometimes they are quiet, sometimes they are dismissed because of one prejudice or another, maybe they are just different or maybe just

112

perceived as ordinary. Undoubtedly, there are those reading this book who are a part of God's hidden people. They are one of God's treasures who will yet be called upon to fit their piece of the puzzle into the Master's plan, a piece that only they can maneuver into place. It isn't that these important people haven't been valiant and doing wonderful, good things all along; it is just that they will have special assignments to perform following the Lord's timetable. God has his great and noble ones concealed throughout the world. They are being prepared. When the time is right, they will step forward and do their parts. God will give them the abilities and help they need to succeed. They will ambush the forces of Satan with great effectiveness.

You need to sharpen your vision so that you don't miss seeing these hidden people. Don't discount people because they are not like everyone else. A person's individuality is a sure sign that a creative God is at work in the universe. Look into the hearts of your sisters in Christ and try to see their true identity. These sisters live now in the dispensation of the fullness of times. They are the great and noble ones, and so are you. Just like Christ and Joseph Smith, Jr., you are learning by prayer, study, faith, and experience to be ready to perform your unique part in the Master's plan when the time is right. You will be called upon to perform many different tasks including rescues of one kind or another. Rescue missions are our specialty.

Chapter 11

Rescue

*"...God, our Heavenly Father, knows each one of us
and generously permits us to see and to share
in His divine power to save."*
Thomas S. Monson[104]

The battle drums beat out the rhythm that calls the righteous to join the fray. It pulses through the world as the Battle Maidens, the Warrior Sons, and all the Saints of God march forth to fight for the liberty of the human spirit. They fight to free the captives from bondage, from the chains of hell. They reach out to grasp the soul smothering in the quicksand of sin, addiction, ignorance, and folly. Gathered about them are their comrades in arms, Christ, angels, family, and the valiant peoples of the earth. Out onto the battlefield they go in their holy quest to rescue the children of God.

The Light of Christ and the Holy Ghost allow the righteous to receive the inspiration and revelation they need to rescue their families, or, through missionary work, to rescue those who search for a better way. The Holy Ghost can visit those who do not have the gift of the Holy Ghost. The Light of Christ is there for all of God's children all of the time. When those seeking truth hear the truths of the gospel, it will sound familiar to them because of the Light of Christ.

114

The Battle Maidens of the Lord

This light is one of the most important ways missionaries have of reaching others with the truth of the restored gospel of Jesus Christ. The Light of Christ in those who teach the gospel reaches out to the Light of Christ in those who hear the teachings, especially if they are not actively quenching the Spirit but have soft, open hearts.

The night is far spent, the day is at hand: let us therefore cast off the works of darkness, and let us put on the armour of light.[105]

The following is a story of rescue, a story of a mother trying to help her child. It could have as easily been a story of missionaries rescuing people from a dark, benighted world and bringing them to the light of the gospel.

THE LESSON

My name is Margaret, and I would like to tell you about my daughter, Pam. During her teenage years she had a feeling that she wasn't as cute as some of her friends. She had gone from the most confident, happy child you have ever seen to an insecure teenager. She did incredible things. Pam was cute, an excellent student, and a gifted athlete. She had many awards, but she felt insecure in her prettiness. Her older sister was the beautiful one that everyone liked. Pam somehow did not feel worthwhile, even with all her accomplishments.

I think that we as parents need to understand that even though a child may have accomplishments, they may be lacking in self-confidence. We need to be alert to what our children may be feeling about themselves.

When Pam started dating in high school, she became interested in a boy named Russell. He was a serious person and very angry. He had had a most difficult childhood. Because of his resentment, he sucked every bit of light and laughter from Pam. Any time I asked her anything about it, she would say that they were just friends. This is a common comment of girls who tell themselves that they are trying to help someone.

I always taught my children to be accepting of all people, to love people. We tried to be kind. They took that principle to heart. I didn't take the next step to teach them to evaluate the people they were dating. I didn't teach them that when you choose a dating partner, you've got to ask yourself if they are loving and giving or if they are takers. Now this was the situation in which Pam found herself. Russell was a taker.

My husband was vehemently opposed to this dating situation. The more he pushed and the more he pried, the more Pam tried to like Russell. I was struggling with his pushiness.

"If you don't back off, you will drive Pam even more toward Russell," I told him. He was not someone I could reason with at the time.

When Pam graduated from high school, she went away to another town to go to college, and Russell followed. Russell and a group of other young people would go over to Pam's apartment every day and just hang out there. We did not feel that this was a good situation for our daughter.

The Battle Maidens of the Lord

Because of my husband's inability to move past his anger, I felt like I was alone. I was devastated and frustrated. Pam would be defensive if I started to talk about the situation. Finally, I realized that there was nothing that I could do to help my daughter. It was hard, so hard. I got down on my knees and pled with my Heavenly Father to give me the words to say because I knew I didn't have them. I asked Him to tell me what I could do to help her. This went on for hours and hours into the night, several nights. I was fasting and praying and pleading with the Lord. Slowly, the impression came upon me that I was to let go and to encourage Pam to encourage Russell to go on a mission for the Church of Jesus Christ of Latter-day Saints. Heavenly Father had Russell's best interests at heart as well as Pam's.

If we didn't change, and they got married, I knew that he would be resentful towards us. Her holding onto him in her co-dependent way would keep him from being able to pull out of his problem childhood. He needed to serve a mission and get out of himself. All of a sudden, I felt that fear and that absolute terror of not being able to help Pam go away. I realized that I had been given an avenue to go down. So that is what I did.

I began to talk to her about being concerned about him as an individual. I knew his anger and his frustration, but I understood where it came from. Kind feelings for him started to come into my heart. Pam began to encourage him to go on a mission. He would have listened to no one else because he relied so heavily upon her. A lot of inspiration came with regard to what

117

Jaqueline Ethington

would help Russell. This was helping Russell and also allowing Pam to think about her own needs. As she turned him over to the Lord, she found herself pulling back. He needed to serve a mission, and he did.

Pam went away to a college in another state where she was able to get a hold of herself and her own goals. She fell in love with and married a fine young man. When Russell returned from his mission, he moved forward with his life. Later he married a lovely young woman whom he loved and who loved him.

It was scary letting go and trusting in God, but it turned out well for both Russell and Pam.

Parents are entitled to insight about the rearing of their children. Sometimes it may come as a flash of unexpected inspiration, but most often the parents will have to ask for the help they need from a loving Heavenly Father. Although Margaret loved her daughter dearly and had her best interest at heart, she didn't get very far in solving what she perceived to be a problem until she began to consult with God. She and her husband simply didn't have the experience, knowledge, or godly love required to deal with the situation, but the Lord did. When the Lord is included in the solution to problems, then they get solved in the best interests of all involved. Prayer is powerful.

In the following story Linda received wisdom and courage to fight for and rescue her son from her community's misguided efforts. She pushed back the evil and held it at bay.

118

The Battle Maidens of the Lord
I HAVE POWER

My name is Belinda, but my friends call me Linda. I have found that the knowledge that God loves me gives me power to change my situation. I have power to change the situation of my children also. For instance, I had been to several Mr. High School Pageants in our town. There were vulgar things said and some vulgar talents displayed. The audience laughed at this crudeness. Being thus encouraged, it became a contest as to who could be the most crude, who could be the most shocking. The adults who should have taken the lead in stopping this, didn't. I have a son who has had some problems with pornography, and he was elected to be in that pageant. Concern about what was going to happen there welled up in me. What questions would he be faced with? What things would he have to view?

Needless to say, I was disturbed. So prayerfully I wrote a letter to the school. In very specific terms I cited just what had happened in past years. I informed them that I didn't feel this should be a community-sponsored event. After that letter, they cancelled the pageant until my son graduated from high school two years later. I was so grateful. I had power to change the situation.

Many of the stories in this book are about rescues of one kind or another. Since the war in heaven, the righteous children of God have been on rescue missions. God sends willing servants out to persuade His children to come to Him. He never sends enforcers; that is Satan's way. Those who try to force their will and way of viewing

119

Jaqueline Ethington

God on others are soldiers in the devil's army. That was the plan Satan presented to the children of God in the council in heaven. Neither Margret not Linda used force. With the infinite wisdom they received from God, the good they desired was achieved.

Chapter 12

Deserters

Behold, there are many are called, but few are chosen.
And why are they not chosen?
Because their hearts are set so much upon the things of this
world....
D&C 121:34-35[106]

The children of God need to hold up their heads. God made the world for them and sent His Son to atone for sin so that they could return to Him after the resurrection. They are more valuable than the human mind can comprehend. Satan wants these valuable beings. He is constantly trying to lead them and their families into a carnal lifestyle. He especially tries to take the youth. He creates an enticing environment in hopes of increasing the number of desertions from the households of faith.

There are deserters. People leave the Church of Jesus Christ of Latter-day Saints for various reasons. Some members of the church become offended by another church member or by a teaching that they either do not understand or will not understand. There are others who find that working in the church is too arduous for them, and they leave to find an easier path. Some members' hearts have been broken because of

121

Jaqueline Ethington

disappointments or perhaps a death or a desertion. They become discouraged and give up hope. Others commit sin and feel badly about it. They become prey to Satan who whispers to them that it doesn't matter if they go to church because all is lost anyway. This is one of Satan's more successful lies. Certain people haven't gained a testimony for themselves and drift away thinking that some day they will come back. After all, their families have been Latter-day Saints for generations. Then there are those who have committed serious sin and have become rebellious.

These rebellious souls are led away by Satan and his servants. Some were led slowly down to hell, and some went dancing and prancing with delight. It was a short-lived delight, but that was the way it started. In these days Satan puts heavy emphasis on sexual sin and pornography. It is designed to lead to desertion from families and from the Army of God.

A lustful desire is the cotton candy that seems desirable at the carnival of life. It looks so enticing. But when it is eaten, it melts instantly in the mouth and is without substance. Satan does his best to entice God's children into infidelity or fornication. He calls out to married people through television and radio for them to find their perfect mate with a free trial to a dating service. He wants to partner them up with the perfect person. These dating services certainly have their place for those who are unmarried. But married men and women have given into the temptation to go online just to see who

The Battle Maidens of the Lord

their perfect match is. Soon they are dissatisfied with the imperfect person to whom they are married.

This dissatisfaction can lead to viewing the ever-present pornography. Satan has it plastered everywhere from billboards and magazines to the internet and television. Some husbands and some wives have been enticed to take a bite of this pornographic cotton candy. They tell themselves that it hurts no one since they view it alone. Thus they begin to dance away from the wholesome life they had begun and follow after the carnival barker that promises a better partner and an easy win at Satan's games. The smiling enticer fails to mention that the games are rigged in Satan's favor. The deceived will only feel like a winner often enough to keep them coming back until they are so entangled in the chains of sin and addiction that they lose all hope of escape. When hope is lost, Satan has almost sealed them his, almost but not quite.

There are deserters who, like the Prodigal son, come to themselves. They finally realize that what they gave up for a seemingly perfect and exciting existence was sweeter and more precious than they thought at the time. They long to return to their families and their God. It may be too late to regain their families, but it is never too late to return to God. "Satan would have you believe that serious transgression cannot be entirely overcome. The Savior gave his life so that the effects of all transgression can be put behind us, save the shedding of innocent blood and the denial of the Holy Ghost." [107] Christ is always waiting at the door listening for that knock. He will welcome his lost lambs back with opened arms.

Jaqueline Ethington

Either the man or the woman can commit infidelity and adultery, but for the purposes of this book, let us look at the situation that many women have to endure. A husband has been unfaithful or is moving toward infidelity. First comes temptation, which, if not strenuously resisted will become an avalanche of desire. Then rationalization will begin, followed by justification in the mind of the adulterer. Once he justifies his actions, he will need a scapegoat. That scapegoat will be his wife. Since he has moved himself into Satan's power, he will begin to follow Satan's program to destroy his wife's inner being. If he can, he will convince her that the adultery is all her fault. Jacob has this to say about unfaithful husbands. *...Ye have broken the hearts of your tender wives, and lost the confidence of your children, because of your bad examples before them; and the sobbing of their hearts ascend up to God against you.* [108] The wife that has been made to feel that the dissolution of her marriage was all her fault is wounded indeed. When in reality, it is her husband's own transgression that has destroyed the union.

The sinful husband will say hurtful and mean things for no good reason other than to salve his conscience. He wants to feel justified in his faithlessness. Once he has sinned, he will lose the companionship of the Holy Ghost and the gifts of the spirit that he had been given. He will say things like, "I never loved you." That doesn't mean that he didn't love his sweetheart with all his heart when they were married. What it means is that because he lost the gift of the Holy Ghost and the gift of love, he cannot remember that pure and holy love that he once possessed for his wife. *And he that repents not, from him shall be taken even the light which he has received; for my Spirit shall not always strive with man, saith the Lord of Hosts.*[109]

Dear and beloved daughters of God, protect and preserve your sacred spiritual core. Do not be deceived by wicked and demeaning words and actions. A marriage is a contract between three people, wife, husband, and God. Only one person has broken faith. The wife and the Lord still have an unbroken covenant. God will give you help through difficult ordeals. Have faith and trust in Him. God will tailor that help for you personally and for your particular situation.

But behold, I, Jacob, would speak unto you that are pure in heart. Look unto God with firmness of mind, and pray unto him with exceeding faith, and he will console you in your afflictions, and he will plead your cause, and send down justice upon those who seek your destruction. O all ye that are pure in heart, lift up your heads and receive the pleasing word of God, and feast upon his love; for ye may, if your minds are firm, forever.[110]

Some husbands may repent and wish to come back to their families. This seems to happen quite often. Then it is up to the wife whether she takes him back or not. Counsel with the Lord about this important decision, and listen carefully to what He has to say. Many women have taken back their husbands and rebuilt a good and trusting relationship. It is a difficult process, but it can be done. In other cases, it may not be a good idea.

Jaqueline Ethington

If things don't turn out happily, when the wife is finally able to forgive and move on with her life without bitterness or rancor, she will once again find peace. If she is at peace, she can find happiness.

This is a simplified and one-sided observation of one type of marriage problem, one type of desertion. Unfortunately, there are wives who do this very thing to their righteous husbands. The presentation of a husband's fall into infidelity is mainly to point out the attempted slaughter of the wife's self-respect that can cripple her life. It is just as great a sin for a wife to attempt to cripple her husband in a like manner. There are also good reasons why some marriages should be dissolved. This sensitive subject should be carefully considered with the help of the Lord.

Of course, there are other types of deserters. There are other covenants that can be broken besides the marriage covenant. Baptismal covenants and temple covenants can be cast aside. The covenant breakers start out well in the beginning. As time passes, they become complacent or rebellious and forget about their promises to God. Satan uses many different ploys to lure people away. Be careful and pray always that you may be called the children of God. The following is the story of a concerted attack by a covenant breaker on a surprisingly strong opponent.

AN ATTACK ON THE FORTRESS

When my parents were married in the temple, my father was a righteous man. I was the oldest child, and

126

my parents named me Nancy. By the time I was two years old, my father had left the church. In the early years, he would permit the family to go to church sometimes. I only remember him with us once. It was on that Sunday when I was about eight years of age that I learned the principle of tithing. It was taught in Sacrament meeting, and it sunk deep into my heart and lodged there. Young as I was, the Lord gave me the great gift of testimony. I knew the gospel was true, that Jesus was the Christ, that Joseph Smith was a prophet. From the few times that I was in Sunday school and primary, I learned the basics of the gospel. My soul soaked up every principle that I heard and treasured it. May God bless those dear teachers and the speakers at Sacrament meetings.

As time went on, my father became more and more belligerent toward the church, and he also fell deeper and deeper into sinful ways. He wouldn't let us children be baptized. We got to go to church fewer and fewer times until Sundays became a horrid day for me. I wanted to be in church but couldn't be. Regular days were fine, but Sundays were barren and bleak. He preached constantly against the church and derided its members.

One day we wanted to say the blessing over the meal as we usually did.

"You ought to be praying to me since I provided the food," my father said.

We all gasped in horror. He, at least, had the decency to look sheepish, and we proceeded to ask the blessing on the food, thanking our Heavenly Father.

Jaqueline Ethington

When I was thirteen, my parents were divorced. I was sad and glad at the same time. My mother, who was a saint, took us to be baptized. From then on we went to church every Sunday. I was never so happy. My father still had a presence in our lives, and my mother insisted that we respect him. She knew that it was important to respect one's parents, and she never said a word against him.

Within a year, my father renewed his efforts to destroy our testimonies and bring us to his way of thinking. He made me read anti-Mormon literature. I remember one book I read which was reported to be the true story of Joseph Smith written by an apostate. It was a most unpleasant book.

A young person has few defenses against a determined and experienced adult. I knew the restored gospel of Christ was true, and I clung to that with all my strength. I became rigid and closed my mind to what I had read. I prayed. I followed the principles of the gospel strictly. I shut out all that threatened and retreated inside to my spiritual fortress. I nursed my testimony, protected it, fought for it, armed myself with it. My battle was real and dangerous. The Holy Ghost stayed by me and helped and sustained me. In the end, my testimony was not destroyed, but my mother lost a third of her children from the knowledge of the truthfulness of the gospel of Christ.

There was a wound in me from that fight. I had a bad feeling about the Prophet Joseph Smith. I tried to shake it, but couldn't. Though I knew he was a prophet,

The Battle Maidens of the Lord

his character had been tainted in my mind by what I had been forced to read. I prayed about it and thought about it often. This was not the way I wanted to feel. Then one day when I was in my early twenties and sitting in a Sunday school class, the Spirit came to me and told me that in the pre-mortal world the Prophet Joseph had been my friend. My heart was filled with a sweet, warm love for Joseph. The reservations that I had had about him slipped away, never to return. What a wonderful gift from God that was.

I sometimes grieved terribly that I had an anti-Christ for a father. My father tried to throw his own children into the fires of hell. Then I remembered that Abraham also had such a father. When God reminded me that He was my Father, too, I was comforted for I have the best Father of all. As time passed, I realized that Abraham forgave his father and took him with him when he fled the land of the Chaldeans. It took time, but I also was able to forgive my father.

There are many children in inactive or part-member families who are forbidden to go to church. But because they have the blood of Israel in their veins, they believe. With the barest of teachings, a part of this group will gain a strong testimony of the truthfulness of the restored gospel of Jesus Christ. Do not neglect these children. Love them and encourage them to come to activities that do not threaten their parents such as activity days, scouting programs, and girls' camp. Encourage your children to include them in their group of friends. There will be a rich harvest among these choice souls. Many will be strong in their testimony of the gospel and their commitment to God and His church because of who they are and what they have had to endure to come unto Him. Remember that these children are not free agents. Do not become discouraged, but treat them and their parents with loving kindness and encouragement. Even though their parents may have deserted God or the church for a time, these children never did. The choice to come to church was never an option for them.

There are various types of desertions from the Kingdom of God. Two examples have been sited here. One is the desertion of a marriage. Another is the desertion of God and the principles of the gospel. Both instances in this chapter are the result of sin. The first and second great commandments were disregarded. *...Thou shalt love the Lord thy God with all thy heart, and with all thy soul, and with all thy mind. This is the first great commandment. And the second is like unto it, Thou shalt love thy neighbour as thy self.*[111]

When people desert the church and fall away, most will eventually come back to the teachings of their God and the church. But there are deserters that don't come back in this life. Fortunately, all is not lost.

Boyd K. Packer tells us that because of the immoral condition of the world today, some of our children may stray from the path of truth much to the dismay of righteous parents. He goes on to say that, "It is my conviction that those wicked influences one day will be overruled... When parents keep the covenants they have made at the altar of the temple, their children will be forever bound to them."[112]

People can desert family, duty, and God, but the atonement of Christ covers all of these situations. He will give aid and comfort now, and either here in this life or in the eternities all will be made right.

Chapter 13

A Field Guide

For behold, thus saith the Lord God:
I will give unto the children of men line upon line,
Precept upon precept, here a little and there a little;
And blessed are those who hearken unto my precepts
And lend an ear unto my counsel,
For they shall learn wisdom...
2 Nephi 28:30[113]

The Battle Maidens presented in this chapter, Georgiana, Kathryn, Suzanna, Alexandra, and Martha, have learned wisdom through their own experiences and inspiration and through observing the experiences of others. They have learned to act with faith and courage. These women are just like most women. At all times they are trying to do their best. Usually they succeed, but sometimes they don't. The example of their lives has earned them distinguished service recognition. Each Battle Maiden's advice is unique to that sister, and each sister has much she can teach.

GEORGIANA
I have learned a lot of things throughout my life. The most important is the knowledge that a loving God lives and knows who I am. That knowledge has been one

The Battle Maidens of the Lord

of my greatest blessings. I remember having spiritual experiences as a child listening to music or just sitting with my Dad or finding something like a leaf where the green has rotted away. It was just a lovely, little, lacy leaf. I was overwhelmed by how beautiful it was and by how much God loved me to make something that beautiful. As I got into my teenage years, the knowledge that my Heavenly Father really does love me, and the respect born of that knowledge, helped me control my behavior. When I was tempted, I knew I would be disappointing a God who loved me. That made a big difference all the way through my life.

When I've had problems and worries with my own children, the first place I wanted to turn was to a loving God. I've tried to help my children have the knowledge that Heavenly Father loves them by finding as many situations as possible where they could feel the Spirit. If I could take them to the temple when the Christmas lights and music were there or take them to a fireside or a church activity, that was my priority. I wanted to put them in a position where they could feel the Spirit so that they would know there was a God who loves them. The testimony that God loves us was knowledge that I felt was important to pass on to my children.

Another thing I have learned about is the importance of time. Sometimes impatience prevents us from overcoming evil. We can be so impatient that we don't allow time for behavior to change or time for attitudes to change. I have a child that has had a problem

Jaqueline Ethington

with an addiction. I wanted the addiction to stop
immediately. It didn't, and I would get frustrated.
Several times in my prayers I have literally had the answer
come to me, "Be patient." It takes time for people to use
their agency and to gain the strength that they need to
overcome evil. Sometimes impatience frustrates the
person trying to overcome sin or addiction. If those
around them can give encouragement and have patience
and allow agency to make that person stronger, then I
think evil can be overcome in time. Time was something
that I, myself, needed when I tried to deal with my father
going in the wrong direction with his life.

Once my father was threatening divorce. I
thought it was for very unworthy reasons. I was angry. I
was extremely angry, so angry I didn't want to be a part of
life or go to church.

One night I remember thinking, "This is crazy. I
can't control my father or my mother. I can't control my
children or my husband. The only person I can control is
myself. And I'm going to stand all by myself before God
at the judgment bar with nobody else to blame. You are
going to have to stand there and be accountable, so get in
gear".

It doesn't matter what is going on. You've got to
control yourself. If anger is holding you up, then you
have to deal with it and get rid of the anger so that it
doesn't affect your eternal salvation. Regardless of
whether it is a parent, spouse, child or anyone who is dear
to you who is not doing right, you cannot let it affect you.
You come against little things that slow your progress.

The Battle Maidens of the Lord

You have to mourn the loss of relationships or sin in someone you love. You have to feel those emotions. But I think it is important that you don't allow those emotions and Satan to succeed in dragging you down.

I have learned that Heavenly Father loves us, that it takes time to deal with problems and to repent and that the only person we can control is ourselves. With this knowledge I can be patient with myself and others and trust in God to do His marvelous work in our lives.

KATHRYN

As a Relief Society President, I have observed many women who have gone through real trials. I have watched their stories unfold and have seen how those who serve others and serve and keep the commandments of God receive heavenly help. Let me tell you about some of them.

Anne Jones and her husband are faithful church members and serve others constantly. However, their children have had trouble getting their lives going in a positive direction. Their son was in a miserable marriage and totally inactive at church, and their daughter's husband had left the church. As Brother and Sister Jones have continued faithfully serving, praying, and keeping the commandments of God, they have begun to see changes in their family. Not everything is perfect, but it is better. Their son is now married in the temple to a different young woman who joined the church. This young couple is creating a faithful, loving family in the tradition of his parents. Their daughter has determined to be active in church and is bringing her children along with her even though her husband hasn't changed. Anne and her husband constantly serve and try to do what the Lord wants them to do. I believe that the Jones' receive God's help with their children's families partly because of their service to others.

Other families in my ward have had similar experiences. Ruth is another example. She has children who have been on drugs and have gone through inactivity. But now her sons are coming back to God. One just got married in the temple, and another is married to a member and is going to church. Ruth is also someone who serves constantly and is seeing results. People who serve others have the help of the Lord.

Another thing that I have noticed is that many people don't go and get the help that they need if there is trouble. Sellina, a sister in our ward, is in her sixties and is just now dealing with sexual abuse from her childhood. She has lived all this time, and now it is affecting her. She is really despondent and suffering and is just now getting help. If you need professional help, don't be embarrassed. Go and get the help you need, and don't wait.

In my own life I learned by watching the experiences of people who serve. I have also observed what happens when you don't get professional help for serious abuse. Hearing about other people's experiences has helped me. "How did you handle it when you went through that trial?" I would inquire. "What did you do," I would quiz. For example, my sister's daughter died from cancer. I asked her how she had handled the trial of the loss of a child.

"Kathryn," my sister said to me, " I knew my life was a fairytale, so perfect. I knew I had to go through trials, so I prepared myself for those trials by studying the scriptures, going to church, and increasing my faith when I had strength. Then the trial came."

One other thing that I have noticed is that some people are embarrassed and don't talk about their troubles, and others are open. I've thought about this and decided it is better to be open. When my brother went astray, my father didn't talk about it. I never knew what my brother did until later in life. He was on drugs, smoking pot, and gambling. Now we all know, but for my father, it hurt too much. My brother is just coming back into church activity after twenty years. If people are more open, everybody can help. Brothers and sisters can pray as well as grandparents and others. What a help it could have been had we all been praying and pleading with God for my brother.

I have learned that the Lord is especially mindful of those who serve others. He will bless their lives and answer their prayers. I have also learned that we often need to get professional help in some instances of abuse and great trauma. Through time I have observed that I can learn much from the experiences of others. Lastly, I have learned that if we will share our troubles with appropriate people, such as our families, we will receive extra help in overcoming our difficulties through their added faith and prayers.

Jaqueline Ethington

SUZANNA

I've had some good times reflecting on how to keep Satan at bay in our homes. I think it is just doing all the little things that you do every day like family prayer, scripture study, and being a good example. Sometimes you forget to have prayer and scripture study, and sometimes you don't have everybody there. It's OK. It is just trying. You're doing your best. I wish I had the magic formula, but I don't. I think it is somewhat different with every family.

We expected our children to be good. We had high expectations but not overly high. When I would go to parent teacher conferences, I wouldn't care so much what their academic scores were. I wanted to know if they were kind to other people. Were they generally kind to others in the class? That was my first question. I wanted them to grow up to be good citizens. There are plenty of people in the world who are smart and plenty of good athletes, but not so many who have a kindness about them. That was important to me.

As the children got older, they struggled with kindness. One child was that way. Even as a young child he demanded more attention, demanded more time and effort. He turned out wonderful, but those third, fourth, and fifth grades were difficult.

I used to tell him every morning before he left for school, "Choose the right, return with honor, do your best, and remember who you are." As I let my children go off to school, I wanted them to know everything I expected of them because I wasn't going to be with them.

The Battle Maidens of the Lord

I wanted them to become kind people and remember what they were supposed to do.

Even with all that teaching, with hopes and dreams for every child to make good choices and good decisions, there is always heartache that comes along. That is what agency is all about. You do your best to teach and guide, and you pray, and you hope that they make it. We always tried to raise our children so that they started making their choices at the right time.

I love Enos in the <u>Book of Mormon</u>. The very first verse talks about how his father brought him up in the nurture and admonition of the Lord. It's beautiful. That is how you raise a family. If you give them too much materially, then they turn out very spoiled, selfish, and difficult. If you give them too much correction and negativity, they fall away from the teachings and values you tried to instill within them. Knowing about these two pitfalls in raising children is important.

We really tried. We had lots of fun, and we laughed and teased each other. We have thick skins. Lots of people don't raise kids with teasing. We are a teasing family, and we get along great. Teasing is something that my husband brought from his family, and I brought from my family. We just don't let little things bother us. I think that is so important. Tough times come along. We try to teach our children to just deal with them.

Being a parent has been an education. As we started out, we were rather inexperienced so we tried to follow the churches guidelines for families by having family scripture study and family prayer. We lived the commandments as best we could so that our children could follow a good example. Kindness in our children was important to us. We avoided giving them too many material things and tried to encourage them rather than giving them criticism and negativism. Instead we had fun and taught them to laugh at themselves and move on.

ALEXANDRA

I was single in a big city for about ten years. Let me tell you some of the things that I have seen.

When I was at work functions, people thought it was weird that I didn't drink liquor. Sometimes they would try to persuade me.

"Just one, take just one drink," they would say.

They thought it was amazing that I had never had a drink in my life.

Some of my former roommates couldn't take the pressure of not drinking. For some reason they were embarrassed that they had different standards. Several would drink liquor rather than say that they didn't drink. Others got into trouble with men, but they never had a word of wisdom problem.

There are a lot of good women out there who have been out of school for a while. Some have had enough of men with pornography problems or moral problems and have just given up. I felt that way, but I didn't give up. Once you start down that dark road, you don't know where it will end. You have to make up your mind about what you want from the start.

The Battle Maidens of the Lord

Here are two things that I saw. One was people who were intentionally and willfully doing bad things because of a rebellious spirit. The second was good people who had become trapped in addictions; they were striving against it, but they were already trapped.

I have a lot more compassion for men who struggle with pornography or same sex attraction. I had never met a man in my life with those problems before I left home. Men don't go looking for porn. It is all around them. I understand some of the effects and how devastating and humiliating it is to women and men. I also have more compassion for those who suffer from same sex attraction. Some brought it on themselves and love it. Others did nothing to bring it on and struggle all of their lives to be released from that burden. Many times I have seen that pornography leads to same sex attraction. Men don't want it, but they don't know how to get out of it. It is a downward spiral. But I have also known some men with pornography problems who have overcome them.

At times women start dating a man and think he is great, and then he hits her with his problems of pornography or same sex attraction. If the women already like him or love him, what do they do? Some work with the man and may eventually marry him. The husbands struggles. Sometimes it works, and sometimes it doesn't. Other women break up with men who have these problems. I have made that decision several times.

I am now sealed in the temple to a good man. If my husband had had any of those issues, I wouldn't have

Jaqueline Ethington

married him. I would have run. Dating men with unsavory problems made me appreciate the good men. There are a lot of fine men to choose from when you are younger, but not so many when you are older. However, I am happy to report that while there are not as many unmarried men, there are not as many unmarried women either. As I have discovered, there are some real gems to be found.

What I've learned is that God is merciful, but he expects a lot from us. He will allow us to make our own decisions so it is important to know what you want. Don't give up on your righteous desires, and be wise in your choice of dating partners. Plan a good life for yourself, one that you will find fulfilling. Then if the right man comes along a little later than you expected, you will have had a good life already upon which to build your marriage.

MARTHA

I have noticed that sometimes people will move into a ward or congregation and within a short time feel like the members are unfriendly. Their lives become sad and self-absorbed. There is a much better way to be welcomed. You need to act. Don't wait around to be acted upon. If you do wait and don't act, Satan may be the one who jumps in there and has his way with you.

First, I ask the bishop for a ward list. Then I proceed to match up faces with names. My husband and I both work on it and compare notes often. We introduce ourselves to as many people as possible and will often find that we have common acquaintances or common interests. I write down these bits of information later and review them until I can remember. We continue to speak to the people we have met while we introduce ourselves to new people. We note the names of those who say the prayers and speak in Sacrament meeting. Before long many of the saints know us, and we have comfortably fit into our new ward. This plan works even for shy people. Neither my husband nor I are very outgoing, but we can do this one step at a time.

I also take cookies over to our neighbors when we move into a new neighborhood. Waiting for people to come to you usually doesn't work. Be brave and have fun.

Another thing that I have noticed is the value of making mistakes. Mistakes can bring you to Christ. There was a time when I thought I was quite wise. I was determined to visit with a certain person about a matter that was important to me. While I was driving to her house, the Spirit tried to warn me not to do it, not just once either. He sat right with me all the way to the driveway, trying to persuade me to stop. But I was fairly young and was sure I knew what I was doing. As you can imagine, it turned out just awful. That dreadful blunder changed my life. Since that time, I have always made a great effort to do exactly as the Holy Ghost directed me. Life has been much better since I was humbled and started listening to the whisperings of the Spirit.

I have learned that things work out better in new situations if I act and do my part in getting to know people. I will be accepted much more readily and learn to

Jaqueline Ethington

love the people I meet sooner. Also, by making mistakes, I have come to know that it is important to listen to the Holy Ghost. Painful experiences can be avoided by listening to that kind counselor.

The women mentioned here have faced sin, trials, and heartache. They have also found goodness, love, and light. Because of their many experiences, they have gained much of the treasured knowledge that God sent them to mortality to learn. Each of us has also learned much in our sojourn here on earth from our own experiences and the lives of others. Just like the women mentioned in this chapter, we are Battle Maidens of distinction. If what we have all learned were gathered into a book, it would be huge and exceedingly valuable.

Chapter 14

The Daughters of Abraham

And I will bless them through thy name;
For as many as receive this Gospel shall be called after thy name,
And shall be accounted thy seed, and shall rise up and bless thee,
as their father.
Abr. 2:10[114]

Because a righteous Abraham asked the Lord for certain things that he greatly desired, the Lord made a covenant with him. This is what Abraham tells us. *And, finding there was greater happiness and peace and rest for me, I sought for the blessings of the fathers, and the right whereunto I should be ordained to administer the same; having been myself a follower of righteousness, and desiring also to be one who possessed great knowledge, and to be a greater follower of righteousness, and to possess a greater knowledge, and to be a father of many nations, a prince of peace, and desiring to receive instructions, and to keep the commandments of God, I became a rightful heir, a High Priest holding the right belonging to the fathers.*[115]

Abraham was seeking the blessing of holding of the Priesthood of God. In the process, he reveals some interesting facts. First, there was greater happiness, peace, and rest through the blessing of the priesthood. Second, the righteous can receive great knowledge. With great knowledge one is able to become even more righteous and receive still greater knowledge. Third, Abraham wanted to become a father of many nations. Fourth, he wanted to become a prince of peace. Fifth, he wanted to receive instruction. And sixth, he wanted to keep the commandments of God.

There is not much that Abraham asked for that his daughters could not also seek. Some of us are Abraham's daughters through birth, and some are his spiritual daughters through acceptance of the gospel of Jesus Christ. Women do not hold the priesthood, but we can have the blessings of the priesthood through the administration of priesthood ordinances. If a woman is righteous, she can ask God for knowledge with the expectation of receiving it. Of course, it is advisable to be wise in that for which we ask. Women can become mothers of many nations just as Abraham's beloved wife Sarah and others did. We can become a princess of peace. And we can desire to keep the commandments of God.

Because of Abraham's righteous desires, he received this blessing. *And I will make of thee a great nation, and I will bless thee above measure, and make thy name great among all nations, and thou shalt be a blessing unto thy seed after thee, that in their hands they shall bear this ministry and Priesthood unto all nations; and I will bless them through thy name; for as many as receive this Gospel shall be called after thy name, and shall be accounted thy seed, and shall rise up and bless thee, as their father.*[116]

The daughters of Abraham are scattered through all nations. If one is not a daughter of Abraham by birthright, she can become a daughter by accepting the gospel of Christ. She can follow his example, and ask for the best blessings. Having the best blessings is a great defense against evil.

Abraham wanted to receive the priesthood of God. Women do not hold the priesthood, but receiving the blessings of the priesthood is not difficult in the nations where the restored gospel has been preached. Baptism and the receipt of the gift of the Holy Ghost is a priesthood ordinance and blessing, one of the greatest. Our baptism leads us to other marvelous priesthood blessings. One such treasure is a patriarchal blessing, which gives us our own personal instructions from God. Another is the temple endowment wherein we are endowed with power from on high. After we have received these priesthood blessings, we can be married in the temple for time and eternity. This is another magnificent blessing that was received by Abraham and Sarah. The power of the priesthood is essential to the salvation of mankind and the operation of God's kingdom on earth. One doesn't have to hold the priesthood to receive the blessings of the priesthood such as baptism, temple endowment and eternal marriage.

As Abraham teaches, knowledge comes in steps or by degrees. About the time a person is baptized through the authority of the priesthood, they have learned the basic principles of the gospel. They have learned about faith, repentance, and baptism. After baptism they then learn more and more until they have a grasp of the basics of Christ's teachings. This is great knowledge, and many

Jaqueline Ethington

people in this world do not have it. If they have become righteous through this process, then things are kicked up a notch. Church members can then receive their temple recommend and go to the House of the Lord where they make their own covenants with God. The temple is a place where they, like Abraham, promise to keep His commandments. When these covenants are kept, the blessings and knowledge received are great indeed. This is greater knowledge. If those who have received their temple endowments continue in faithfulness and desire and seek for greater knowledge, the Lord can shower it upon them. This knowledge is received through studying the scriptures with greater understanding, through learning gained from messages of prophets, apostles and other church leaders and their writings, and through revelation from the Holy Spirit.

In the following scripture, the Lord tells us just how much knowledge He is willing to give us. ...*It is given unto many to know the mysteries of God; nevertheless they are laid under a strict command that they shall not impart only according to the portion of his word which he doth grant unto the children of men, according to the heed and diligence which they give unto him. And therefore, he that will harden his heart, the same receiveth the lesser portion of the word; and he that will not harden his heart, to him is given the greater portion of the word, until it is given unto him to know the mysteries of God until he know them in full.*[117] The "he" and "him" in this scripture are generic terms like "mankind." Women may also know these things. Probably few of God's children have received all knowledge, but many have received more

148

The Battle Maidens of the Lord

than is common through the ministrations of the Holy Ghost..

Knowledge is one of the gifts of the Holy Ghost. *God shall give unto you knowledge by his Holy Spirit, yea, by the unspeakable gift of the Holy Ghost....*[118] The knowledge that can be received is not just what is called spiritual knowledge. For example, although Carrie had no mental handicaps, when she was about thirty years of age, she felt like her mind had been trapped in a cage from which she couldn't break free. It seemed to her that a ceiling had been placed on her ability to understand many things that she wanted to know. She prayed mightily for some time to have this limit removed. Eventually, she could feel her mind soar and has since gained the desired knowledge and developed talents and abilities that had previously seemed beyond her.

Abraham wanted to be the father of many nations. We can desire to be the mother of many nations. Remember that the twelve tribes of Israel all started with Abraham and Sarah's one child, Isaac. Children and grandchildren are a magnificent force loosed upon the earth. In a thousand years, we, too, may be the mothers of many nations.

Another of Abraham's desires was to become a prince of peace. Some of the people that the devil hates most are Abraham's daughters who become princesses of peace. If a woman has a desire to become a princess of peace, she can actually be one. It is not easy and has to be worked at. Human nature being what it is, self-serving and egotistical, being a peace maker has to be a deliberate choice. There are certain things that have to be given up. One example of things that will need to be put away is storytelling of the wrong sort, gossip. When a woman is telling a really good story at the expense of someone else, everyone's eyes are riveted upon her. The storyteller is the center of attention, and it is a heady experience, to say the least. If someone tries to divert this low behavior in others, the participants in the gossip session will sometimes turn on her like a pack of snarling dogs. The listeners don't like to give up the delicious bone they are chewing on. Be prepared. A person determined to be a peacemaker has to know who they are and where they are going. Pray for tact, a gentle nature, and great courage.

If we have made the decision to be a princess of peace, how do we go about it? Actually, it is akin to having charity or the pure love of Christ. It is a process to get there. One way would be to pick out one or two things to work on at a time, like being kind and looking for the good in people. The pure love of Christ is a spiritual gift, but it won't be bestowed lightly. Only those who sincerely desire it and work hard to develop Christ-like traits will be granted that gift. But we are the children of Abraham, and it is within our power to become peacemakers if we truly desire it. Be patient with yourself. Time limits don't apply here. By continually renewing your efforts, you will move forward toward your goal. Almost anything can be accomplished one step at a time.

Abraham's posterity has the responsibility to carry the gospel to the world. How do we do that? A few of us

The Battle Maidens of the Lord

will go on missions to preach the gospel. One way for those of us who don't go on a regular mission to bring others to Christ will be by our examples. By example, we show others what it is to belong to the Church of Jesus Christ of Latter-day Saints. We have all also been asked to be member missionaries, to share the gospel when we have the opportunity, or when we are prompted by the Holy Ghost to do so. For example, once when flying on a long trip across the continent, I sat next to a young man studying to be a rabbi. I couldn't help myself. I turned to him and said, "Hi, cousin. I'm from the tribe of Ephraim." We spent the next two hours in an amiable discussion of the wonders of the restored gospel of Jesus Christ. We talked about Jerusalem and temples, prophets and priesthood. He was especially interested to know that there was a prophet upon the earth. I don't know if he pursued his interest in our conversation, but I felt the Holy Ghost there, and I think he felt it, too. We have these kinds of experiences sometimes, but our families will be where the majority of our work will be done.

Mostly the Battle Maidens of the Lord, those great daughters of Abraham, will be engaged in teaching their sons and their daughters the gospel and passing on to the next generation their heritage of righteous service, their heritage of godly knowledge, their heritage of the gospel of Christ. Some of the daughters of Abraham will not have children, but will have the opportunity to teach others these things their entire lives. Women are the main purveyors of culture and heritage from generation to generation. This is an essential job, not one to be taken lightly. Women are a vital part of Heavenly Father's plan for the salvation of mankind. The Battle Maidens are indispensable in preparing for the establishment of Zion upon the earth and in preparing the earth for the second coming of Christ in glory.

The daughters of Abraham can participate in all the blessings promised to his righteous descendants. Like Abraham and Sarah, we have a work to do. As Abraham once rode out with his men to save his nephew, Lot, the Battle Maidens also have to go on rescue missions to save their own families and others in the family of God. Where much is given, much is expected. We, as women of the last days, have come to earth with missions to perform. We must stand fast in the gospel cause and not be moved out of our place. God will help us and send angels to walk with us. We are not alone.

Chapter 15

Hannah's Long March

He raiseth up the poor out of the dust...
To set them among princes,
And to make them inherit a throne of glory;
1 Sam. 2:8[119]

Battle Maidens have been coming to the earth periodically from the beginning of time. Since the restoration of the gospel of Jesus Christ by Joseph Smith, many have come and will continue to come to perform the urgent work of salvation now underway. Hannah, a daughter of Abraham, was one of those great souls. She set an example of faith, courage, and steadfast determination that few could surpass. She was a princess of peace and a mother of many nations or at least tribes. As a child, Hannah walked across the plains with the pioneers. When she grew up, she and her husband were one of the many faithful couples who helped turn parts of the untamed western North American continent into the bountiful garden it is today. Hannah returned to her Father in Heaven in December of 1928 and is buried in Colonia Jaurez, Chihuahua, Mexico. This is a part of her story as written in her autobiography. There is much here that can be learned from her about the character of Battle

Maidens and the varied nature of the battles that they will have to fight while upon the earth.

Parley P. Pratt brought the gospel to her family in 1842, the year Hannah was born. They soon left Canada for Nauvoo, Illinois. As a child, Hannah heard Joseph Smith preach and always remembered what he looked like. On the day she saw Joseph Smith, her father took her up to the top of the unfinished Nauvoo Temple and showed her the beautiful view of the Mississippi River. It looked like an ocean to her.

In the winter of 1846, her family, along with the saints in Nauvoo, were driven out of their homes by mobs and sent to wander in the wilderness across the Mississippi River. At Winter Quarters her mother died of exposure and hardship. Her father left the following spring for the Salt Lake Valley to find a home for his family, leaving Hannah, her sister, and brother with relatives.

In 1849, her father sent for the family. Little seven year old Hannah was excited to start on what she thought was to be a pleasure trip. Because her aunt was busy, she traveled with strangers on the day the wagon train started for the West. To Hannah's dismay, the strangers chopped off her beautiful long hair. With tears in her eyes, she walked beside the wagon. Hannah traveled without shoes for her feet or a hat for her head the whole long, weary way to Salt Lake, a journey of over fifteen hundred miles. Sometimes they traveled two or three days without water. In Emigration Canyon her father met the family with vegetables and melons from his garden. It was a joyful reunion.

The Battle Maidens of the Lord

Hannah grew up happily with friends and family in Salt Lake City, Utah. In May of 1862 she married in the Endowment House the love of her life, Miles. In June of 1862, her husband left for his mission to England. Hannah wrote, "We had no display at our marriage, nor a very long honeymoon, but our love was for each other, and we were happy in each other's society. The day we separated I felt that the only friend I had had left me. I was twenty years old when I was married, and my husband was only nineteen."

Miles was released from an honorable mission after three and half years, and their life together started in earnest. Miles was a faithful church member and calls from the Prophet Brigham Young took them to various places the Western United States. Each assignment took them further and further south.

In 1881, the family was called to go to Arizona to help settle St. Johns. It was a rough place, and the local settlers were prejudiced against the church members. After a while, Miles went to Salt Lake to ask President Young to send more settlers. When the new people arrived, things got better for a while. However, a short time later, he was asked by his church leaders to go to Mexico on an urgent mission. Hannah promised to meet him there with their children and worldly goods. In her autobiography she tells the story of that trip.

"In March of 1867, I started for Mexico with seven children and two wagons and teams of horses. It had been snowing in the mountains for about three weeks before I left St. Johns. I expected company to go with me

155

from St. Johns to Mexico, but when I went to see Brother Skousen, he was not ready to go, so I started out alone. When I got as far as Nutrioso (high in the White Mountains), Brother and Sister Pace...insisted on my staying over for several days.

"Brother Pace said, 'Hannah, aren't you crazy, starting out on this journey with your small children? Did you know that Geronimo, the renegade Indian chief, is on the warpath?

"I told him I guessed I wasn't afraid, so I would have to start on this journey and trust in our Heavenly Father to see us to the end. My son, Will, took a job herding stock for some of the ranches, so he did not go with me.

"Brother and Sister Pace were very kind to us. She had me bake bread, and make cookies, and gave me butter and meat, etc., to use on the journey. The first night after we left Nutrioso, we camped in a beautiful grove. It snowed all night, and in the morning the boys built a fire, and we dried our bedding. We had some terrible roads to travel over, snow and mud often up to the hubs of our wagon. One day a blizzard started, and it got so cold I wrapped the smaller children in their bedding and made them as comfortable as I could. Then I got out and walked to keep warm. We saw a ranch house (a small cabin used only seasonally) in the distance, so we made for that point. The boys went in and built a fire while I took the children in and got supper. I made the boys' bed in the house and then took the larger children and slept in the wagon. I got up several times during the night to see that the children were all right. When I got up in the morning, there were icicles on the water barrels a foot long. After breakfast we hitched up our team. We did not know a mile of the road.

"That night we got to Apache Hill about sundown. One of the boys went ahead and returned saying it would be almost impossible to get down the mountain that night. So I carried all the bedding I could and loaded the children with enough provisions to last us. Miles, my son, thought he could get down with one team. So the boys cut down a tree and chained it to the back of the wagon to keep it from tipping over. I took a lantern and went ahead to light the road. When we got to a level spot on the mountain, it was about ten o'clock, and I thought we had better camp.

"I got the children supper and put them to bed. I sat there considering our condition—way off in the mountains camping right on an Indian trail. I assure you I did not do much sleeping, but the Lord protected us. In the morning the boys went back to the top of the mountain to get the other wagon we had left there. When I saw them coming down the mountain, I held my breath, but they got down all right without breaking even a singletree. That day we traveled on and struck the Frisco River (an Arizona river is generally like a stream any place else). It ran through the canyon for miles and miles. We crossed that river forty-one times.

"The next day I thought we had better camp, bake some bread, do the washing, and rest the horses. The following day we came to a hill about a mile long that was solid rock. When we got to the bottom, the horses, not having been shod, were unable to get a footing on the rock and, consequently, could not pull the wagon three inches at a time. We unloaded the wagon and pushed on the wheels, trying to get the horses to pull it up the hill. But they could not make it move. All this time I was praying in my heart the Lord would open the way for us.

"We did not know there was any human being within miles. Finally, we heard the sound of wagons, and rounding the bend of the road there were several coming with three or four span of mules on each wagon. When the men drove up, they swore at us and ordered us out of the road.

"I went and talked to them telling them our horses were not able to take the wagon up the hill. They were U.S. soldiers who had been gathering supplies for their camp. The captain rode up when he heard what I had to say. He ordered the men to unhitch their mules and take our wagons up the hill. I had a sack of cookies, and I doled them out to the men. I was so thankful they had helped us out of our difficulty.

"We traveled on for several days having bad roads and more cold weather. Just before we got to Williams Valley, there was another long dugway (a road dug out of a mountain or steep hill). We could not get down on account of some mining men who were hauling their machinery to another part of the country. We had to wait the biggest part of the day. While we were waiting, one of the men asked me where we were going. I told him, and he looked around the wagon.

158

The Battle Maidens of the Lord

"Is this all the firearms you have," he said.

'Yes," I answered.

"Are you thinking of going through Indian country with nothing to defend yourselves?" he asked.

"I told him I needed no defense from man as I was trusting in the Lord to see us safely to the end of the journey.

'That night when we camped, I would not allow the boys to make a fire, as I felt that Indians were all around us. In the morning we found remnants of bows, moccasins and other things that indicated Indians had recently camped there. "When we got to Williams Valley, I expected W.C. McLellan to go with me into Mexico, but he was not ready and wanted me to wait two weeks. I asked him if he could find work for my boys and team. He could not, so I told him we would have to go on. He tried to get a man to go with us, but there wasn't a man in town who would consent to go, as the Indian problems were bad. Three men and three horses were killed three days before on the road we had to travel. I told them we would trust in our Heavenly Father to protect us, as I had all the boys and teams my husband had, and he needed them to put in a crop.

"When we camped at noon, my boys took the shoes from the horses that the Indians had killed as our horses needed them. I sat up all that night with the baby in my arms, fearing the Indians might come. I was thankful when morning came. I didn't let my children know I was frightened. The next day while walking, I picked up a paper that had been printed in Silver City

159

Jaqueline Ethington

(New Mexico) the day before, warning the people to be prepared, as Geronimo and his men were in that part of the country. That worried me, but we never saw an Indian on our journey."

Hannah and her family spent many years in Mexico living by faith and hard work. In faith she walked out into the dark on a road of which she knew not one mile. Heavenly Father supported her feet and led her to safety through perilous country in dangerous times. Since she did not have enough food for the journey, the Lord sent her into the hands of the good Pace family who provided her with bread, butter cookies, meat, and other necessities. While they were traveling high in the White Mountains, the Lord provided them with a warm ranch cabin during a spring blizzard. When she and her boys had done all they could do to get up the rocky hill, the Lord sent the cavalry riding out of the pines to her rescue. Hannah's journey was approximately four hundred and sixty-five miles long, part of which was over what is today called the Coronado Trail. It is a winding road that snakes through some of the most rugged country in the Western part of the United States of America. She was never intended to make this trip alone, but the men and families that Miles had arranged to go with her wouldn't go. I suspect that Hannah had to make this journey when she did because she did not have any means to support her family while her husband was in Mexico. And Miles truly did need their boys, the horses, and the farm equipment that Hanna was bringing in order to provide for his family.

The Battle Maidens of the Lord

Hannah fought the battles of her life with courage and faith. We can do the same. She raised a faithful family, and her numerous posterity have carried on the traditions of gospel service and obedience. As a descendant of Abraham and Sarah, she and the righteous members of her family were and still are entitled to the blessings of and the right to hold the priesthood, spiritual knowledge, posterity either in this world or the next, and every other blessing associated with the covenant the Lord made with Abraham. Hannah's trials were great, but she pushed forward with the courage that comes from knowing that God was with her. She lived her life well and made many sacrifices so that she would be able to abide in glory in the celestial kingdom with her family, her Heavenly Father and her Savior, Jesus Christ.

Chapter 16

Marching Forth to Glory

Lift up your hearts and be glad, for I am in your midst,
And am your advocate with the Father;
And it is his good will to give you the kingdom.
D&C 29:5[120]

The battle of heaven and earth is the battle between good and evil. It is the battle in which the Battle Maidens of the Lord have been engaged since the War in Heaven when Lucifer tried to take over the throne of the Father. Lucifer failed, and now he is trying to tempt as many of the Father's children as he can into sin. He wants power over them. Power is what he has always wanted. However, in the end, power is not what Lucifer will have.

Satan has tempted some of the Father's children to desert Him and the principles of righteousness. The Father's children who follow evil and do not repent will have to pay for their own sins because they would not take advantage of the atonement made for them by Jesus Christ in the Garden of Gethsemane. One can be any kind of sinner, except for those who sin against the Holy Ghost, and if they repent, they will be forgiven. The Battle Maidens have helped recover many of these sinners, especially those in their own families. Satan, his

162

companions from the pre-mortal world, and his converts in earth life are the adversaries of the Battle Maidens. How will these enemies fare when judgment and mercy have claim on them after they leave mortality?

There are those whom Satan deceived on earth who delight in their favorite evil and never repent. Their hearts are hard, and they do not accept the Gospel of Christ or have a testimony of Jesus (D&C 76:82). There is nothing as hard as a heart of stone, and to write upon such a heart, the Lord must use a hammer and chisel. And so the unrepentant are thrust down to spirit prison to receive their tutorial.

The disobedient will have eternal punishment, or in other words, God's punishment.[121]   They will have to pay for their own sins. When Christ paid for our sins, the pain was so great that He sweat great drops of blood. Those who have to pay for their own sins will have to endure that exquisite pain. The unrepentant will not be able to leave spirit prison until they have paid for all of their sins by themselves.   Satan will be permitted to torment them for quite a long while after death. That is an awful price to pay when repentance and forgiveness are available to all. But these disobedient earthly children—Satan's tools on earth--will have a glory beyond understanding, even though they will be compelled to pay a high price for it.   After the disobedient are finished with their arduous task of settling the debt for sin, they shall be assigned a kingdom of glory and be heirs of salvation.   They will go to the telestial kingdom where they will receive the ministry of angels and the Holy

Ghost.[122] The glory of this kingdom is like the glory of the stars.[123] As the stars differ in glory, so shall the resurrected bodies of these people differ in glory. *And thus we saw, in the heavenly vision, the glory of the telestial, which surpasses all understanding.*[124]

All will eventually evade Satan's grasp except those who have a "perfect knowledge of the divinity of the gospel cause, a knowledge that comes only by revelation of the Holy Ghost, and then link themselves with Lucifer and come out in open rebellion."[125] These are called sons of Perdition. Perdition is another name for Satan or Lucifer. There are very few who could even be in danger of the sin against the Holy Ghost. Of those who could, such as prophets or apostles, few would.

Satan, whom the Battle Maidens have fought since the War in Heaven, doesn't win.[126] Even Cain, who gained a body, rules over Satan. The Lord said to Cain, *If thou doest well, thou shalt be accepted. And if doest not well, sin lieth at the door, and Satan desireth to have thee;...and it shall be unto thee according to his desire. And thou shalt rule over him; For from this time forth thou shalt be the father of his lies; thou shalt be called Perdition; for thou wast also before the world.*[127] As we know, Cain did not do well. When he murdered his brother, he fell into Satan's power and became Satan's ruler.

All those who accepted the Plan of Salvation and joined with Christ in the pre-mortal world will get a body and be partakers of salvation. They will receive a kingdom of glory with the few exceptions already mentioned.

The Battle Maidens of the Lord

The children of God who live the higher law—those who are the good and honorable people of the earth but who will not accept the fullness of the restored gospel—will receive a higher kingdom and much greater glory than those of the telestial kingdom. These are they who inherit the terrestrial kingdom. They will *receive the presence of the Son...*[128] The glory of their kingdom is like the glory of the moon and much greater than the telestial kingdom, which glory passes all understanding. These good people will have a heaven much like the one they are expecting. There will be no marriage there as many anticipate. The 'death till we part' section of their marriage vows will be in force as they thought. For reasons that seem good to them, these people will be unable to accept the fullness of the restored gospel when it is preached to them by God's great missionary force after this life. But they have earned an excellent reward, and they will be happy.

Those who accept the restored gospel, receive the saving ordinances, and keep the commandments of God, will receive exaltation in the celestial kingdom. There will be many who will not have the opportunity to receive it on this earth and will be taught by missionaries in the spirit world after they die. If they accept their message, then the saving ordinances will be performed for them on earth in one of the temples. Among the numbers of those included in the celestial kingdom will be the Great Battle Maidens of the Lord and the Valiant Warrior Sons of God who have remained faithful. The glory of their kingdom is like the glory of the sun.[129] These people will accept baptism by one having authority as well as the gift of the Holy Ghost. They will receive temple ordinances. Their marriage in the temple will be eternal, and their family will live forever in perfect felicity, emulating their Father in Heaven and His family. Glorious!

The Battle Maidens' mission is to bring as many of God's children with them to the celestial kingdom as they can. The battle between good and evil that started so long ago in another realm goes on. The Lord sent us here at this time because we are strong, and we can do the vital work of helping our eternal brothers and sisters return to our Heavenly Father. Have faith and trust in the grace of Christ to make up for anything you feel is lacking. Perfection is not possible in this life so do your best and pray for and expect help from God. That help will come in surprising ways. The truth is that we, with Christ, win. Righteousness always wins in the end. Light always prevails against darkness. *He that overcometh shall inherit all things; and I will be his God, and he (they) shall be my son(s) (and daughters).*[130] We are God's children, and He will own us as such when we return to him having fought valiantly against evil here on earth just as we did in heaven.

And so it is plain that the plan of a loving Father and His Son, Jesus Christ, was designed to lead to glory and even exaltation; that agency was a blessing, not a curse. The only ones who receive no glory are those who were cast out of heaven for rebellion, and those few who have a perfect knowledge of the Plan of Salvation and then rebel against God here on earth. The rest of the Father's children are marching forth to glory.

CHAPTER 17

A Review of the Troops

He (She) that overcometh,
The same shall be clothed in white raiment;
And I will not blot his (her) name out of the book of life,
But I will confess his (her) name before my Father, and before
His angels.
Revelation 3:5[131]

The Battle Maidens of the Lord are the great spirits who stood with their companions, the Warrior Sons of God and Jesus the Christ, in the War in Heaven. They went in among those deceived by Satan to persuade their brothers and sisters to follow the Plan of Salvation that was designed to lead to glory and even exaltation. Many courageous Battle Maidens have now come to earth to fight in the last great battle against evil. They are here to bring about the righteousness that will lead to the establishment of Zion and the return of Christ.

Most of these daughters of God and their husbands are creating homes where Heavenly Father's faithful children can be raised and taught correct principles. One of their greatest missions is to protect and preserve their families and bring them to Christ. Those who are not engaged in child rearing have other missions to perform.

Jaqueline Ethington

Christ and the Holy Ghost are always close to the Battle Maidens. These valiant women do not walk alone but are surrounded by angels who are sent to protect and help them in their vital missions here on earth.

We are the Battle Maidens of the Lord. God has given us power to do a great work. It is in our natures to have strength; sometimes it is a quiet strength, and sometimes it is not so quiet. It is in our natures to be brave and courageous deep down in that eternal part of our being. We have fought evil with our companions since the War in Heaven. Christ led his armies to victory then, and He leads the daughters and sons of God to victory now.

We Battle Maidens have powerful enemies, but we have been given effective weapons against them. We walk in the Light of Christ with the companionship of the Holy Ghost and are never alone. With faith in Christ, we can do all things that are needful in the fight against evil—in the fight to save our families as well as our eternal brothers and sisters. By keeping the commandments of God, we keep Satan from having power over us, and we can teach our families to do the same. We follow the example of our beloved brother, Jesus Christ, and our righteous ancestor, Abraham. God has given us spiritual gifts to help us in our battles. When we rely upon God our Father, His Son, Jesus Christ, and the Holy Ghost, we will never be abandoned. God will present us with difficult tasks to perform thereby letting us grow and stretch in our abilities, but He will never leave us.

168

The Battle Maidens of the Lord

We, the Battle Maidens of the Lord, have learned many important principles from our experienced and righteous sisters. Here are a few of the valuable lessons of life shared by the sisters who contributed to chapter 13, "A Field Guide."

God loves each of us.

Repentance takes time.

The only person that we can control is ourselves.

Service to others brings the blessings of heaven.

Get help if you have been sexually molested or abused. Don't wait or be ashamed to ask for it.

Learn good principles from others' experiences.

To raise a good family, keep doing all the little things we are taught to do on a regular basis. Have regular family prayer, family home evening, family scripture study, and go to church.

Teach children to be kind.

Bring children up in the nurture and admonition of the Lord.

Decide early in life to follow Christ and don't get off track.

Follow the commandments and keep out of Satan's power.

Stay far away from pornography.

God is merciful, but in His wisdom, He expects a lot from us.

Act, don't wait to be acted upon.

Mistakes are great teaching tools to bring people to Christ.

Jaqueline Ethington

The Battle Maidens have missions to perform here upon the earth. The Lord will give each person experiences to qualify them for these missions, and He will give them the talents needed to perform them. Often they will have to take a step out into the dark, but He will take their hand and guide their footsteps.

There are those who desert their posts by becoming inactive for a time or by following after Lucifer's battle plan. However, many of God's daughters, His Battle Maidens, are firmly grounded in the gospel of Christ. The women of the latter-days have their boots on the ground fighting for the preservation of their families in righteousness. They are teaching their children to keep the commandments of God and to fulfill their missions here upon the earth. The Battle Maidens are becoming a Zion people and also teaching others to fulfill that role in order to prepare for the coming of Christ. *Wherefore be faithful; stand in the office which I have appointed unto you; succor the weak, lift up the hands which hang down, and strengthen the feeble knees. And if thou art faithful unto the end thou shalt have a crown of immortality, and eternal life in the mansions which I have prepared in the house of my Father.*[132]

You Battle Maidens who now walk upon the earth by faith, put on the armour of God, take up the stick of righteousness, and go forward in courage with faith, hope, and love. You are not alone. Do not be afraid. Lean upon the steel rod that is your testimony of Jesus Christ. If that rod is slender, you need only band together with the rods of others, and it will become unbreakable. Do

170

The Battle Maidens of the Lord

good and fear no evil. Prepare for the coming of the Son of Man. Follow the example of Christ, daughters of Abraham. You are glorious.

Christ our Redeemer, Savior, and King, be Thou with us.

Sources Cited

Books

(13) (86) Joseph Smith Jr. *Teachings of the Prophet Joseph Smith,* Compiled by Joseph Fielding Smith, Salt Lake City, Utah, Deseret Book Company, 1974.

(20) Seumas MacManus. *The Story of the Irish Race,* Greenwich, CT, Konecky & Konecky in cooperation with The Devin-Adair Company, 1921.

(40) (80) *The Prophets Have Spoken,* compiled by Eric D. Bateman, 3 Vols., Salt Lake City, Utah, Deseret Book Company, 1999.

(56) (125) Bruce R. McConkie. *Mormon Doctrine,* Salt Lake City, Utah., Bookcraft, 1966.

Magazine articles

(17) Spencer W. Kimble, *Ensign,* Nov. 1979.

(50) Spencer W. Kimble, Conference Report, *Ensign,* Apr. 1978, p 123.

(52) Ezra Taft Benson, *Ensign,* Jan. 1991.

(62) L. Tom Perry, "The Great Plan of Our God," *Liahona,* Feb. 2009, pp 62-66.

(67) Dallin H. Oaks, *Ensign,* Jan. 1995, pp 7-8.

(68) Boyd K. Packer, *Ensign* ,Feb. 1993, pp 7-13.

(71) Boyd K. Packer, *Liahona,* Apr. 2005, pp 8-14.

(90) Bruce R. McConkie, *Ensign*, Jan. 1979, p 61.
(96) Dallin H. Oaks, *Ensign*, Sept. 1986, p 68.
(107) Richard G. Scott, "Finding Forgiveness," *Ensign*, May 1995, p 75.
(112) Boyd K. Packer, "Our Moral Environment," *Ensign*, May 1992, p 68.

Scripture References

<u>The Holy Bible</u>

(1) 2 Kings 6:16
(2) Rev. 12:7-9
(7) Rev. 12:9
(9) Isaiah 6:8
(12) 1 Thes. 5:19
(14) 2 Tim. 1:7
(24) John 13:15
(25) Matt. 4:3
(26) Matt. 4:4
(27) Matt. 4:5-6
(28) Matt. 4:7
(30) Matt. 4:8-9
(32) 2 Cor. 11:14
(35) Matt. 4:10
(37) Matt. 26:41
(38) 1 Cor. 110:13
(39) 2 Pet. 2:9
(42) Matt. 4:11
(44) Psalm 91:11-12

(55) John16:33
(57) 1 Pet. 5:8
(58) Ephesians 6:12
(60) John 16:33
(73) EX. 31:3
(75) Acts (:31
(76) John 14:26
(77) 1 Cor. 2:13
(78) 1 Pet. 1:21
(82) John 14:21
(84) Phil. 4:8
(91) Joel 2:28
(92) Acts 2:18
(93) Rev. 19:10
(100) Joshua 1:9
(101) 2 Tim. 3:1-7
(105) Rom. 13:12
(111) Matt. 22:37-39
(119) 1 Sam. 2:8
(123) 1 Cor. 15:40-41
(126) Rev. 20:1-3
(130) Rev. 21:7
(131) Rev. 3:5

Book of Mormon

(11) Moroni 1:19
(16) 2 Nephi 32:5
(19) Alma 17-26
(29) Alma 30:48

(43) 1 Nephi 11:18
(47) Alma 56:48
(54) 1 Nephi 14:14
(59) Moroni 7:16-17
(65) Jacob 2:8
(66) Jacob 32:3
(70) Moroni 7:19
(74) Moroni 7:44
(79) 2 Nephi 32:5
(81) 1 Nephi 15:24
(83) 2 Nephi 10:23
(85) Alma 32:21
(89) 1 Nephi 7:12
(95) Alma 32:23
(98) Moroni 7:33
(108) Jacob 2:35
(110) Jacob 3:1-2
(113) 2 Nephi 28:30
(117) Alma 12:9-10

The Doctrine and Covenants

(3) D&C 76:25
(10) D&C 138:29-30,38-39
(16) D&C 10:5
(18) D&C 82:18
(21) D&C 65:2
(22) D&C 108:8
(23) D&C 98:1-3
(30) D&C 121:39
(36) D&C 20:22

(42) D&C 84:88
(45) D&C 138:55-56
(46) D&C 93:36-37,39-40
(48) D&C 18:15-16
(49) D&C 97:21
(51) D&C 105:5
(52) D&C 1:35
(61) D&C 27:15
(63) D&C 29:6
(64) D&C 18:34-36
(69) D&C 95:8
(72) D&C 88:6-7,11-12
(94) D&C 93:24
(97) D&C 27:15-18
(106) D&C 121:34-35
(109) D&C 1:33
(118) D&C 121:26
(120) D&C 29:5
(121) D&C 19:66-12
(122) D&C 76:88
(124) D&C 76:89
(128) D&C 76:77
(129) D&C 76:70
(132) D&C 81:5-6

The Pearl of Great Price

(4) Moses 4:1-3
(5) Moses 4:4
(6) Moses 1:1-39
(8) Abr. 3:27

(33) Moses 5:13
(34) Moses 7:26
(88) Moses 1:12-22
(102 Moses 6:31
(103) Moses 7:13
(114) Abr. 2:10
(115) Abr. 1:2
(116) Abr. 2:9-10
(127) Moses 5:23-24
(133) Abr. 3:22

About the Author

Jacqueline Ethington graduated from Arizona State University with degrees in education and home economics. She has worked with young women in schools and church. As a Relief Society President and diligent church worker, she has aided and counseled many women throughout her life. She and her family reside in Arizona.

www.ingramcontent.com/pod-product-compliance
Lightning Source LLC
LaVergne TN
LVHW051056080426
835508LV00019B/1911